HISTORIC FAYETTE COUNTY

An Illustrated History

by Carolyn Cary

Commissioned by the Fayette County Chamber of Commerce

Historical Publishing Network
A division of Lammert Incorporated
San Antonio, Texas

CONTENTS

First Edition

Copyright © 2009 Historical Publishing Network

ISBN: 9781935377030

Library of Congress Card Catalog Number: 2009928269

Historic Fayette County: An Illustrated History

author:	Carolyn Cary
cover artist:	Vicki Turner
contributing writers for "Sharing the Heritage":	Britt Fayssoux
	Joe Goodpasture
	Carolyn Cary

Historical Publishing Network

president:	Ron Lammert
project manager:	Violet Caren
administration:	Donna M. Mata
	Melissa G. Quinn
	Evelyn Hart
book sales:	Dee Steidle
production:	Colin Hart
	Glenda Tarazon Krouse
	Craig Mitchell
	Charles A. Newton, III
	Roy Arellano

PRINTED IN SINGAPORE.

THE HISTORY OF FAYETTE COUNTY

THE VERY BEGINNING

Imagine, if you will, 20,000 years ago. The Northern Polar icecap began to get colder and colder, and began to draw moisture up out of the oceans to keep it cold.

This condition reached a point where the Aleutian Islands stretched south from Alaska all the way to South Russia-North China.

After several hundred thousand years of exploring Earth we hominids were a curious bunch and decided to see how far this new land extended. And they began walking northeastward.

When they got to Alaska, (I always use present place-names) some of them said "ooh, too cold for me" and proceeded down through Canada, Washington, Oregon and California.

They traveled in small family groups, or bands, as it would be easier to feed a small group. However, they stayed within a few miles of each other, in case of trouble.

They proceeded down through Central America and South America. Some of the bands said "ooh, too hot for me" and traveled northward through Texas.

The only way of obtaining meat was to tie a stone or piece of quartz that had been shaved into a point onto a stick and go running into a deer or a bear. Needless to say, they often went hungry.

Though they only lived into their 30s, every day was spent walking and searching for food.

Those indigenous travelers eventually reached Georgia approximately 12,000 years ago.

DETERMINING THEIR TIME OF ARRIVAL IN GEORGIA

Have you ever wondered just how archeologists determine that a particular site is 12,000 years old?

It has to do with the carbon content in living things. Oddly enough there is the same amount of carbon in our human bones as there is in the tree outside your window.

After death, every 500 years a set percentage of carbon leaves the bones or the tree trunk. All archeologists have to do is determine how much carbon is left in their site discoveries, and the age is thus determined.

Starr's Mill is the third mill building on this site. It ceased being used in the 1950s and is now owned by the county as a pumping station site.

In our early schooling, we learned that the United States was settled from Plymouth Rock west to the Pacific Ocean. Not so.

Our native Americans came from the west to the east. And yes, they were still walking every day hunting food.

If you have lived in Georgia for very long, you have discovered the fact that it has many rivers, creeks, and tributaries. The hot summers would dry up the creeks, and leave some nice squishy ground in which our early settlers realized certain foods, such as squash, could be planted and harvested.

Thus they began to become agrarian, remaining in place for at least 3 or 4 months of the year.

By 1540 ACE our original Georgians had really gotten the hang of farming and staying in one place permanently.

Fernando De Soto was traveling northward from Florida through the middle of Georgia, looking for gold. Because he found the Indians living beside the creeks, he gave them their name of the "Creeks," a name still in effect for those Indians who lived in two-thirds of Georgia, from the Chattahoochee River southward.

THE CREEK INDIAN NATION

English and Spanish settlers had been settling along Georgia's Atlantic shores for over a hundred years. The Creeks could see the advantage of permanent housing, and had developed their own code of laws.

In the mid-1700s three brothers named McIntosh arrived just south of Savannah. One of them, William McIntosh, would travel up through Creek territories as a salesman.

In 1776 the state of Georgia only extended just north and south of the City of Savannah. All the rest was Creek Nation territory. As McIntosh traveled through what we believe is now Carroll County, he met Senoya He-ne-ha, a Creek Indian princess. She was of the "Wind Clan" which was akin to the upper social strata of the day. Yes, the town of Senoia in Coweta County was named for her.

They married and had a son, William McIntosh. Although he was really a "junior" that term was never applied to him. He was

accepted in both worlds for the early part of his life; his father saw he was well educated in the white world and his mother saw to his Creek education.

By the time he was nearly grown, however, more and more of the Creek lands had been sold and were now part of the state of Georgia.

Around 1818 he had built a home at Indian Springs, which had been a stopping-off site for the Creeks for over a thousand years. It was on a trail that went from Augusta, Georgia, to Talladega, Alabama.

McIntosh senior had now returned to Savannah, and McIntosh junior was Principal Chief of Coweta Town. It is now known as Columbus, Georgia. The title held the same meaning as being a mayor. He next became Principal Chief of the Creek Nation, akin to being the governor.

By 1820 almost all of the Creek Nation had been ceded to the state of Georgia. Technically the Principal Chief had the right to cede or sell land without consulting the various tribal chiefs.

In 1821 the state of Georgia approached Chief William McIntosh about purchasing the tract of lands extending west to Line Creek. Those Creeks in Georgia were referred to as the "Lower Creeks" and those that inhabited the eastern third of Alabama were called the "Upper Creeks."

Chief McIntosh called all the various Creek representatives together at his summer home in Indian Springs, near Macon, to discuss the matter. His farm home was in Whitesburg, Carroll County, on the Chattahoochee River.

Every great leader has a nemesis, and his was a man named Menawa. He was a member of the Upper Creeks and did not have the advantages of understanding both the white and Indian worlds that McIntosh had. He just knew there wasn't much Creek land left in Georgia and he was vehemently opposed to losing any more of it.

However Chief McIntosh prevailed and it was decided to cede the land that became Fayette, Henry, Houston, Dooly and Monroe counties in January, 1821.

Needless to say, Menawa returned to Alabama not the least bit pleased. Just four years later, the last of the Creek Indian lands

Opposite page: Chief W. E. "Dode" McIntosh, great-great-grandson of the Creek Indian chief who was assassinated in 1825, also served as chief from 1962 to 1972. Here he visits Peachtree City, Georgia, as it builds an amphitheatre in 1976 to put on a play about the assassination.

in Georgia were ceded, creating the counties of Lee, Muscogee, Troup, Coweta, and Carroll. At this time the Creeks were walked to new Indian Territory that later became Oklahoma. Chief McIntosh' son, Chilly, would lead the first "Trail of Tears" to Oklahoma in 1827 and 1829.

On the way home from the 1825 treaty, McIntosh's son, Chilly, believed the last words out of Menawa's mouth after the meeting, that he would kill McIntosh for ceding these last lands in Georgia. McIntosh replied that he didn't think going into hiding was necessary and that surely his own people would not take his life.

MENAWA TRIES TO HAVE THE LAST WORD

Menawa and perhaps as many as 100 Upper Creeks were hiding in the woods on April 20, 1825, near McIntosh's home in Whitesburg. They were intent on taking his life and assumed this would end once and for all the loss of Creek lands. McIntosh, who was age 50, his son, Chilly, age 30, and sons-in-law and friends were coming home from hunting about 2 o'clock in the morning.

Now it was an Indian belief that if you were going to take your enemies life, you had to take it on his doorstep, or you wouldn't go to Indian heaven. Consequently Menawa let them all get home and into bed before making a ruckus. They burned the barns, slaughtered mules and horses and then set fire to the house.

McIntosh had told Chilly that if any trouble did come, however, he should dress himself and the youngest son in the house, Daniel, age 2 1/2, in women's clothes and get down to Line Creek to Alexander Ware's house.

Trouble was indeed upon them and Chilly and Daniel managed to escape. When the house was burned to the point that Chief McIntosh had to come out of it, he was shot and finally he fell. It was an Indian belief that if your enemy was going to take your life, he couldn't just leave you there to die—and the two wives of McIntosh implored Menawa to finish what he started. He stabbed the Chief and the miscreants scattered in every direction.

The wives then started towards Peachtree City and were met halfway by Chilly and Alexander Ware. They all stayed here until the first Trail of Tears in 1827 to Indian Territory.

The wives also wrote a letter to Georgia Governor George M. Troup and it is dated May 1, 1825, Fayetteville, Fayette County Georgia, asking for help. Now, the governor of Georgia was indirectly related to Chief Mcintosh and he didn't want anyone to know this, so he took several months before getting funds and munitions to Ware to pursue these killers.

MENAWA FINALLY GETS THE PICTURE

In 1834 Menawa could see that the Creek lands in Alabama were being ceded and they would be marched to the Indian Territory. He wrote: "Here are the hands that are stained with the blood of McIntosh, and I am now ready to stain them again in the blood of his enemies…when I done the deed I thought I was right, but I am sorry."

FAYETTE COUNTY IS CREATED

Fayette County was created in January, 1821, and is the 49th county created in Georgia. It was also the smallest of the five created, only being allowed four districts. Along with the lands in Henry, Houston, Dooly, and Monroe, the new territory was carved up into 202 1/2 acre squares.

At this time, Fayette County went up above Atlanta, over to the other side of Jonesboro, and south into what is now Spalding County. Of course, what the state giveth, the state can taketh away.

In 1828 and later in 1870, land from Fayette was taken to create Campbell County, which is where Fairburn and Union City are now. It went in with Fulton County in 1932.

A portion of our land was taken to create DeKalb County in 1822, a portion was taken to create Spalding County in 1851, and a portion was taken to create Clayton County in 1858. Our boundary has been the same since that time.

WE GET A NAME

Because a number of those drawing land lots and settling here also had to choose a name for the new county, it is conjectured that those who fought under the French General Marquis de LaFayette, gave us his name.

LaFayette was born in 1757 and was the only child of a long-serving military family. When he was only two years old his father was killed in the Battle of Minden, fighting the English.

He was reared by an aunt and grandparents, as his mother preferred to stay at the courts in Paris.

He graduated as a captain from military school about the time of the American Revolution. While he loved his king and queen, Louis XVI and Marie Antoinette, he also admired what was going on across the pond. Since he was of the second wealthiest family in France, and his wife, Adrienne de Noailles, was of the wealthiest, he gathered up men and supplies and sailed off to America.

He presented himself to General George Washington in Philadelphia and his first major engagement was at the Battle of Brandywine in Pennsylvania in September, 1777. He was badly wounded in the knee and was attended to by Quakers for several months.

He served in other military engagements and was at Yorktown for the surrender of English General Charles Cornwallis. Needless to say, Cornwallis would only give a sword of surrender to Washington, who was in New York City and had to ride his horse pell-mell to Yorktown.

LaFayette was only 20 years old at this time.

However, it is not a stretch to say that some of the hundreds of Revolutionary veterans drawing land here had fought under LaFayette at one time or another.

A COUNTY SEAT IS CREATED

FAYETTEVILLE

In 1823 the State of Georgia decreed that each new county must create a county seat, and it must be equidistant in the county. Looking at the present map, Fayetteville is not equidistant in the county. But at the time is was chosen, given our vast size in 1823, it was centrally located.

In March 1823 the Inferior Court decreed that Land Lot 123 was the center of the County.

Because the lot chosen to build the courthouse on was on property drawn by Joseph M. Post, District 5, Land Lot 123, it had to be purchased from him. He was to receive $800 and was paid $100 to begin with. The balance would come from the sale of lots.

Larkin Bell was employed for $30 to lay out lots in this land lot with each size to be sixty feet on the front, going back 120 feet. Streets were to be laid out at eight feet wide.

The lots were then sold at an average of $20 each, which had to be paid by December, 1823 or lose whatever down payment they may have made.

In 1823 a contract to build a temporary courthouse was given to Simeon L. Smith who had bid $78. He was to have it completed in four months, and it would have been a small wooden building.

It is interesting to note that in 1823 the city of Fayetteville covered 3.4 square miles and in 2008 it covered 10.98 square miles.

In December 1824 M. Bosworth was paid $898 to build a jail, and in April 1825 the plans were drawn up for a permanent courthouse.

❖

The Courthouse Square about 1970. The price of gas on the gas pumps is 39 cents a gallon. In 2009 all this is gone and a jewelry store operates out of the remodeled gas station. In the 1920s, a bank was in the building.

FAYETTE COUNTY COURTHOUSE
Fayetteville, Georgia

Right: The Fayette County Courthouse was built in 1825 and is the oldest courthouse building in Georgia. It was originally two stories, and in 1965 was made three stories.

Below: On Easter Sunday, April 11, 1982, 10:35 p.m., two men, who had a criminal trial coming up the next morning, broke in, went up to the third floor, poured nine gallons of gasoline on the wooden judges stand, and threw a firebomb into the area. It was rebuilt and here the new cupola is raised onto the top of the tower. They served 18 months of a five year sentence.

The county seat was governed by the county commissioners until 1889 when the first election was held for a mayor. Capt. W. P. Redwine was elected to this office. However, as a part of the enactment creating this new governance, neither the mayor nor the five councilmen were to receive any salaries.

Capt. Redwine died in September, 1890. He had led one of the first volunteer groups during the War Between The States.

The value of an eight-year old cow in 1872 was $10, in 1909 it was $40, and in 1916, it was $90. In trying to ascertain the price of a cow on the hoof today, one could get over $800. Of course the cows today are sold when younger and are much meatier.

All males over the age of 16 and under 50 years of age, and who had resided in Fayetteville over 10 days, had to work the streets and roads not more than 15 days year, or pay $5 in place of working. If they would do neither, they could be fined $2 a day for each day's default or have to work 10 to 30 days extra that year.

The 2008 population in Fayetteville is 15,327 folks, 1,422 commercial businesses and 310 homes.

In the county in the 1800s there were 37 known doctors and in the early 1900s to the 1960s, there were 16 known doctors.

As of this writing, there are well over 500 doctors practicing in the county. Some, though, are here only one or two days a week.

THE COURTHOUSE

Finley G. Stewart bid the lowest for this building, and was paid $1,764 to begin construction. By the time it was completed in

1831 there had been a total of $8,000 spent for its completion.

About 1860 it was decided to put up a "neat fence." The posts were to be 10 inches square and were to be sawn or hewn out of post oak or heart pine. The railing was to be three inches square and to have two coats of white paint. The posts were to be placed two feet in the ground and there were to be three gates. One William Wilkerson was paid $275 for this "neat fence."

In the 1880s the clock tower was added but it was 1909 before a clock was added. It operated by weights and pulleys until 1953, when it was electrified.

Until the very early 1900s, there were homes on the south side of the Courthouse, where businesses are now. The people who lived in the homes decided they wanted to say they faced "the front of the courthouse" so the tower end has since been referred to as the "front of the Courthouse." In reality, it's a moot issue.

Interestingly, the Courthouse was firebombed in 1982 by two criminals who had a criminal trial coming up. The cost of putting it back together was $1.2 million dollars.

The Fayette County Historical Society sold T-shirts that said "I helped rebuild the Courthouse" and many companies donated labor to help in its restoration. The original 1825 bricks that had fallen to the ground were sold complete with a gold plaque on top.

While we can no longer call it "The Courthouse" due to our new Justice Center, we can still brag that it is the oldest courthouse building in Georgia.

We are privileged to have this building still in existence and while it is no longer used to hold court, it is used for the Fayette County Chamber of Commerce and the Fayette County Development Authority.

Above: The Fayette County Historical Society was formed in 1971 and various past presidents are from left: Ed Bradford, Tony Parrott, Bobby Kerlin, Carolyn Cary, Ted McAuliffe, Lamar McEachern, and John Lynch. Taken in 1995.

Left: The Fayette County Courthouse was built in 1825 and has seen the number of county residents grow from 5,555 in 1830 to 106,000 in 2009.

THE EARLY SETTLERS AND FOUNDING OF FAYETTEVILE

A lottery was held to settle the new counties. Each county, with its district numbers and land lot numbers, was each put on a piece of paper and put into, if you will, a fish bowl.

They were to lay out a jail, a courthouse, and to fix the site of public buildings. They were to create Captain's Districts with two Justices of the Peace to be elected in each Captain's district. We now refer to these districts as GMD's, or Georgia Militia Districts. There were nine originally laid out, and those nine are still legally in place. They were used as voting

Schoolchildren delight each Halloween bringing their pumpkins to the Courthouse Square.

If you were a veteran of the Revolutionary War, you were allowed two draws. If you were a widow with minor children, you got two draws, etc. There was a list of about seven instances in which you were permitted to draw. And, oh yes, there were blank pieces of paper in that fish bowl.

It was 1822 before several hundreds of settlers were here. Each successful drawer was given a 202 1/2 acre tract of land for a filing fee of $19.00.

Most settlers were farmers and since all the land lots were now given out, the county began in earnest.

The Georgia Legislature of 1821 appointed temporary Justice of the Inferior Court, now called the County Commissioners, and those appointed were: James Strawn, Thomas A. Dobbs, Richard Respass, J. M. C. Montgomery, and Jesse Harris.

districts but due to the increase in the number of citizens residing in the county, those nine have been subdivided into 36 voting districts within those original nine.

The Captain's Districts or the GMD's were the first National Guard units, that each state has now. Men were ordered to turn out each Saturday morning with the their guns and practice various military maneuvers, "just in case."

These temporary justices were to also see that elections were held to elect a Clerk of Inferior Court and Superior Court, a Sheriff, a Coroner, a Tax Collector, a Receiver of Returns of Taxable Property and a County Surveyor. By and large, these offices are still viable ones.

Early names in the first ten years of the county include, in addition to those already mentioned: William Morgan, Alexander Ware, James Alford, Allen Post, John H. Rooker, James

Head, John Caldwell, Henry B. Thompson, Eldridge Millsaps, and Eldoridith Kitchens,

Andrew McBride served as one of the first constables and among the first Justices of the Peace were John Thompson, James Mebrick, William Harkins, and Aquilla Hardy. John Welch served as the first sheriff in 1822 and Winston Wood served in 1823 and 1824.

The state legislature of 1824 enacted a law authorizing the Justices of the Inferior Court to purchase land for the Fayette County Academy and to turn the land over to the trustees of the academy. Those trustees named were James Head, Wiatt Heflin, Jordan Gay, William Gilliland, Sr., and Finley G. Stewart.

We do not have any more specifics on this academy nor the Female Academy chartered in 1834. We do have information on the academy chartered in 1855 and that information is to follow.

CENSUS RECORDS

The first census held in Fayette County was in 1830, and it showed that 5,555 citizens resided here.

If you take the mean average of citizens over the next 140 years, from 1830 to 1970, it is 8,000 people. It was up a little here and down a little there but averages 8,000 folks.

It went down in the 1860 census due to Clayton County being formed and the state took Jonesboro from us and gave it to Clayton County. It went down again in the 1930 census

due to the boll weevil hitting our main crop, cotton, in 1921 and the sharecroppers had to leave and find work elsewhere. Automobile production in Detroit was increasing, and many headed in that direction.

From 1970 to 2008, the number of our residents rose from a mean average of 8,000 to 106,000 people.

EARLY COST OF GOODS

The average price of goods in our first 40 years included $2.50 for six sitting chairs, one set of knives, forks and knife box was $1.50, one sifter and two bread trays were $2, two feather beds were $75, one sorrel horse was $45, and 12 head of cattle would go for $65 in the 1820s and 30s.

In the 1840s eggs were 12 1/2 cents a dozen, a pair of cotton stockings was 75 cents, a vial of castor oil was 37 1/2 cents and a yard of calico could be purchased at 50 cents. A set of buttons were 37 1/2 cents, two cow hides would go for 15 cents, a plug of tobacco sold for 50 cents, and a pair of suspenders were $2.99.

In the 1870s, five mules were worth $1,000, 17 lbs. of butter fetched $4.25, and six sides of leather could bring $24.00.

FAYETTE COUNTY IN THE MID-1800s

Businesses in the City of Fayetteville at this time included two churches, both of which

The train tracks were laid down through Fayette County's east side in the 1880s. They were taken up in 1939. The depot was used as a restaurant for many years and in 1986 it was moved across the street. It now serves as Fayetteville's Tourist Center.

are still viable, two schools, three stores, five bar rooms, a printing office and a division of the Sons of Temperance, which probably prevented having more than five bar rooms.

The Legislature enacted a law enabling the Tax Receiver and the Tax Collector to visit the homes of each widow for the purpose of affording them a better opportunity of being able to pay their taxes. It was decreed that no widow should be returned as a defaulter.

An academy was chartered in Tyrone with Charles Smith, Franklin Landrum, Jarrot Handley, M. J. Smith, and G. R. Sims being appointed Trustees of Hopewell Academy.

John D. Stell moved from the county with his family to Texas but many of his family descendants still reside in Fayette County.

The value of all the real estate in the county in 1850 was set at $2,185,835. Today it is $9,757,305,200 dollars and yes, that's "B" as in billion.

One Jared I. Whitaker, a prominent Fayetteville attorney, served as a Justice of Inferior Court and was the Clerk of the Baptist Church in Fayetteville. He moved to Atlanta in the mid-1850s and became its 16th mayor. He also was the proprietor of a newspaper, "*The Atlanta Intelligencer*," forerunner of "*The Atlanta Constitution*."

An act was passed preventing the sale of spirituous liquors within one half mile of the Courthouse in the town of Fayetteville. If you did so, the fine was set at not less than $500, or imprisonment in the common jail. However, it did not prevent the sale of said liquors by physicians for medical purposes in any quantity.

In 1855 Colonel James F. Johnson, who was married to the former Martha Holliday, aunt of the famed "Doc" Holliday of western fame, sold a piece of land to the trustees of the newly formed Fayetteville Academy. This was the beginning of a school on this site until about 1967. The Fayetteville City Hall is located on this site at the present time.

One of author Margaret Mitchell's aunts and grandmother attended this academy. The aunt's father, Phillip Fitzgerald, lived on south McDonough Road, in part where the Thames Dairy is located. The southern portion of Fitzgerald's land is now located in Clayton County.

If you have a copy of the original publication of "Gone With The Wind," look on page 4, and you will find Scarlett O'Hara attending the Fayetteville Female Academy. The original 1855 academy, however, was always co-ed.

It has been rumored that Martha Holliday Johnson was not happy living in Fayetteville, where she grew up, and wished to be somewhere where the social scene was dominant. So her husband helped to create Clayton County in 1858 and they moved to Jonesboro. Their house is still in existence there.

WE HAVE PRODUCED TWO GOVERNORS

Two of our native-born sons have become governors. In the late 1860s, William Hugh Smith became the governor of Alabama.

He was born April 26, 1826, the son of Jeptha Viven and Nancy Dickson Smith. His maternal grandfather, David Dickson, was a general in the Georgia Militia and had served in the American Revolutionary War. Dickson was buried in an area which was in Fayette County at the time (now is in Clayton County). The Smith family moved to Alabama when William Hugh was 11 years old. He died in Birmingham on January 1, 1899.

The county provided six companies of infantry who fought primarily in Virginia and Maryland with some fighting in North Carolina and Florida. There were two companies of cavalry that were associated with State Guards. By comparison, this county provided 330 men in World War I and 599 in World War II.

❖

Left: The Holliday-Dorsey-Fife House was built in 1855 by Dr. John Stiles Holliday, uncle of the "Doc" Holliday of Western fame. It is now a city museum.

Below: In 1929 several ladies in Fayetteville started a library. It grew into the Margaret Mitchell Library, named with her permission, in its own building in 1948. They are from left, Mattie Lena Blalock Ingram, Louise Culpepper Murphy, Laura Thornton, the librarian, Lucille Alladio Busey, Lucy Reagan Redwine. Photo c. early 1970s.

Hugh Manson Dorsey was born in Fayette County on July 10, 1871. He received his elementary education in Fayetteville but his family moved to Atlanta when he was nine years old.

He was admitted to the Georgia Bar and practiced law until he was elected governor of Georgia in 1916. He served as a judge of the Superior Court of Fulton County in 1934, remaining in this position until just prior to his death in 1948.

THE WAR BETWEEN THE STATES

The War Between the States, a.k.a. The Civil War, began in the Spring of 1861.

There were 5,000 people here, and 2,000 fathers, brothers and sons entered the Confederate Army.

Fayette County provided nearly 1,500 of its finest and about 400 of these did not return.

The only action on Fayette County soil came in July 1864, when some Union soldiers were coming our way from Palmetto during the night. They happened upon a long Confederate supply train stretched out nearly two miles long on Highway 54, beginning about where Bennett's Mill is. This building has been a restaurant for the past several years.

Above: A Confederate veterans reunion took place at the Courthouse in Fayetteville, c. 1900.

Below: This Confederate flag was made in Fayetteville, February 1861. It hangs in the Georgia State Capitol. Second from left, John Lynch and Carolyn Cary.

The wagons with supplies and payroll for Atlanta were burned and many horses and mules were slaughtered. The Confederate soldiers were garrisoned on the Courthouse Square. Due to increased skirmish activity in Jonesboro, many were let go and others taken to Lovejoy.

The next day the situation was turned around and Confederate soldiers were chasing Union soldiers through the Inman community, and at Ebenezer Church Road and Ebenezer Road a day-long skirmish took place.

Known as the Skirmish at Shakerag, both sides suffered many casualties before a Confederate General, Joseph Wheeler, led a headlong charge that broke the Union lines. He captured Union officer Lt. Col. Robert Kelly, and about 200 of his men, routing the rest.

Leaving the wounded with local Fayette County families in this area, Wheeler continued his pursuit of the Union soldiers toward Newnan, where the Battle of Brown's Mill ensued. General George Stoneman was captured at Brown's Mill.

When returning soldiers came home in 1865 they found their personal property missing or destroyed, their farm stock was gone, and their money was worthless. Many were crippled in some way from fighting but they all managed to rebuild their lives by the one thing they all knew best—hard work.

Nineteen years later several Fayette Confederate veterans got together and formed an association in the Hopewell community of Tyrone. In 1908 a railroad was established coming up the west side of Fayette County and directly through Tyrone. This Confederate veterans association grew in time with many veterans coming from the surrounding counties to participate. Many who did not otherwise have a family requested to be buried in the Hopewell Methodist Cemetery, along with many of their comrades.

AFRICAN-AMERICANS IN FAYETTE COUNTY

Early indications seem to say that a larger number of blacks did not appear until the early 1830s. Farming was the main occupation and after the War Between The States many left the farms for employment in the larger cities.

Some stayed here though, working on the farms or sharecropping. As early as 1868 Jordon Price owned 138 acres of land valued at $900. Others had livestock and household goods valued as much as $300 and one man had $800 worth of farm animals and personal belongings.

Records of 1877 show they owned 1,882 acres valued at $7,965. In 1909 there were 15 families living in the county paying tax on tracts of land varying from one acre to 155 acres. After this period of time in the 1900s most records no longer distinguished white from black ownership in tax records, census records and marriage records.

The Fifteenth Amendment, passed in 1870, gave the vote to Negro men. However Reconstruction laws as well as community customs discouraged them from voting. Many were illiterate and that was one of the requirements to vote.

Speaking personally, I came to the area from Ohio in 1959 and when I registered to vote I had to both read and write a paragraph.

The churches and schools have been the greatest influences in the lives of the people of color here.

Fayetteville native, Arthur Arnold, was the county's last living blacksmith. His grandfather had been captured as a 10 year old in Virginia and brought to Fayette County.

In 1977 there were eight Baptist churches in the county, six Methodist churches and one Church of God In Christ. Their beginnings date as far back as 1854. Most are still viable congregations.

There are a number of descendants from the original slave families still residing in the county. They served or are serving as school teachers, real estate salespeople, working in the county administration office and construction.

FAYETTE COUNTY HAS ITS SESQUICENTENNIAL

❖

In 1971 this committee put together the county's sesquicentennial, its 150th birthday. Starting at the bottom, C. J. Mowell, Jr., Helen Teague, Carolyn Cary, Albert Berg, Francis Reeves, Kathryn Langford, Aline Ellington, Edwin Ellington, Hubert Langford, Joan Busey, Dorothea Redwine, and Helen Woolsey.

In the fall of 1970, myself and C. J. Mowell, Jr., realized that Fayette County would be 150 years old. We gathered about 20 other citizens who were interested in the county's history, and worked for 5 months to put together an event unheard of here before.

It was also realized that the counties of Henry, Houston, Dooly, and Monroe would have

that distinction as well. So work began in earnest but very quietly.

Newly elected governor, Jimmy Carter, was asked to open the event on June 26, 1971. He brought along his daughter, Amy, who was three years old.

We had created an 8-day event and a part of it was an opening day parade, and a driving tour around the county. Maps were provided.

Interestingly, during the parade on opening day, I was holding Amy, when my own three-year old came by on a float. When she saw me holding another little girl, her look would have stopped a swiftly running river.

The other seven days were filled with such activities as a play about Chief William McIntosh at the Fayette County High School, the uncut film of "Gone With The Wind" at the Sams Auditorium at the school, and the Third Army Band concert on the Courthouse Square. Senator Herman Talmadge delivered a speech here, and at the end of it, a helicopter released 200 red carnations down into the square. A total of over 10,000 visitors shared this event with us.

VARIOUS OLD COMMUNITIES

Fayette County has always had communities with some interesting names.

There's Shakerag for instance. It's in the western part of the county and while no definitive explanation has been given, it is suggested that during an election some time in the mid 1800s, a fight developed between two men over a political disagreement. When the fight was over, one man had thoroughly thrashed the daylights out of the other and had torn off most of his opponent's clothing. The defeated gladiator ran home, and, as a signal of victory, the triumphant one hung the remnants of clothing on a very conspicuous bush to blow in the breeze. It is one of the original nine Militia Districts.

One of the original families in Shakerag was the Leach family. This family still resided on the same land when Peachtree City was created in 1959. More on Peachtree City in a separate history.

As in all small communities in the 1800s, there was a syrup mill that was originally owned by the Leach family and lastly by G. O. Tinsley, the name we now call it. A portion of the original mill sits for all to see on the golf course in Peachtree City.

The original Kedron was a post office and store in the mid to late 1800s. It sat on what is now Highway 54 at the Fayette-Coweta county line. Due to rural mail carriers not existing yet, the store owner would get the mail from the post office and keep it at his store for the "one stop" shopping convenience of his customers.

Aberdeen is a township built about 1900 on what is now Highway 54 at the Aberdeen shopping center.

It was a rather bustling community with four stores, a cotton gin, and, after the railroad went through about 1908, it had a depot with a local agent on hand. At this time that railroad is the only one operating in Fayette County. The railroad tracks in Fayetteville were taken up in 1939.

The current area in Peachtree City called "Clover" is exactly where the original community sat about 1908.

In 1916 there was a depot, store, and gin house here. In 1918 "Mr. Dave" McWilliams bought the store and later moved it to what is now Highway 54 on the western edge of Peachtree City. It contained the usual items, plus mule-drawn farming tools. He operated the store until his death in 1977. A relative has said that his uncle kept all his money in a croker sack, a heavy burlap bag that would have been used to ship seed or fertilizer in.

Starr's Mill is associated with a mill built in the south end of the county about 1822 or so. It is named for one of its millers. No explanation has been confirmed as to why his name stuck and others have not, but it is possible that Hilliard Starr owned the mill in 1866.

At one time there was a cotton gin that served the community. It was a huge rambling structure and operated by the same type system as the mill, which was by gates that opened and shut on each end of the dam. This provided the proper flow of water to drive the machinery. It is said that when it was no longer used as a gin it became the hangout for local boys. It is also said

that it was the site of quite a few poker games and beer parties. I declare!

It sits within the Glen Grove community and the only explanation given is that it was named for "Old man Glen."

Another name for the area in the early 1900s was Nyson although there is no explanation for where the name came from.

Old Dublin sat just a half mile north of Starr's Mill. It was a viable community until the War Between The States. It contained the Gaulding Masonic Lodge, all of whose members had to serve in the Confederate Army. The minutes of the lodge in 1862 state "meetings were suspended in consequence of the *War! War! War!*."

This community was never able to become viable again.

Rest was also a community near here. Once again, no reasonable explanation can be found. One theory held that the postman came this far south, rested, and returned back north.

If you travel down the current Highway 85 connector to Brooks, and hang a right, go down a hill towards a creek, and you will be in the early 1900s community of Chestlehurst.

It became a viable community due to the railroad traveling through there and the fact that the dirt by the creek made really good bricks. In fact it made so many bricks, there is a huge lake there now.

It was quite a rough and tumble community about 1905 or so. It was rumored that unwanted citizens were shot and then strapped to the railroad tracks. There was only one store and when it was purchased, the first owner built one across the street. Then he sat on its porch with

❖

Starr's Mill and Gin House has existed since the 1820s. The first mill building was built in 1824, this current building is the third one on the site. Only the foundation of the gin house remains.

a rifle shooting around anyone attempting to go in that first store!

W. B. T. Gordy, locally renowned potter, is said to have flagged down the train one day. The conductor told him "Get on board quick because I don't want to stay in Chestlehurst any longer than I have to."

A word of warning, however. The property is now owned by some men in Atlanta who use the area for hunting.

Whitewater is shown on a map of 1847 and would be located just about where the White Water Baptist Church is located on 85 Connector. It seems to have had a post office from 1850 to 1871. Note: the name is spelled as one word or as two words.

Black Rock is one of the original nine Militia Districts. Located in the northern part of the county and as did all like communities, it contained a blacksmith shop, smoke house, a gin mill and syrup mill.

The first church is Black Rock was the New Hope Baptist Church and it is still a viable congregation.

Cross Roads was a community where Fayette and Clayton counties come together. One of the very first settlers was Drury Banks, a veteran of the American Revolutionary War.

The Banks family cemetery, dating back to 1870, is still in existence.

The current subdivision known as Rivers Edge sits near the site.

As we have seen, early communities all had a store, a gin, and a church. Flat Creek is no exception. It sat about five miles east of Fayetteville and it still contains the Flat Creek Baptist Church, one of five constituted in the 1820s, which is still a viable congregation. More can be learned in a separate history of churches of the 1800s.

Fife is an old community, supposedly without a particular name until the railroad was put through about 1908. This is also the same railroad through Clover, Aberdeen, Peachtree City, and Tyrone.

Fife is just above Tyrone and had the prerequisite store, blacksmith shop, barber shop, post office, It sits at the Fayette-Old Campbell, now Fulton County line.

It had a larger than usual commercial district, probably because of the railroad, and it even had a bank in the 1920s.

In the 1930s watermelon shipments were the biggest enterprise going. This was also true of the community of Woolsey, named in a later history.

The watermelon shipments, had as many as 70 car loads leaving Fife each day in peak years.

Because the communities of Fife and Bethany sit on two county lines, it has been rumored that some of its citizens believed they lived in Fayette County. However, when a few received tax bills from Fulton County, they paid them, not wanting to stir up any confusion. No matter who they paid their property tax bill to, they felt they were still Fayette County citizens, shopping in Fayette County and sending their children to Fayette County schools.

Bethany's history is really a duplicate of Fife's, and also sits along the railroad. The Bethany Methodist Church and cemetery reside sit at the center of the old town.

Harps Crossing, located on South Highway 92, was obviously settled by Harps in the mid-1800s. It was and still is a thriving residential community. There are still Harps living here.

From the early 1900s an interesting story has been passed on is about the fish fries held here. It had an annual event held just after spring planting. The men would fish most of the night on Whitewater Creek and then heated up big black pots to cook the fish in.

The women would come the next morning with the necessary picnic types of food.

It's "sister" town is Inman, just a mile further down the highway.

The land was soon settled after the Land Lottery Draw of 1821, and the first to come were Stubbs and Hills.

Because the community was small and close-knit, and transportation so poor, activities had to be in each other's home. Needless to say, marriage took place between neighbors, and as can be stated about all of our original communities, it was best not talk about anyone because they could be related to the person you were talking to.

A railroad was laid down by this management crew in 1907. It was laid down through Peachtree City and Tyrone, and is still in use.

Inman enjoyed its first store in 1884, opened by Daniel McLucas. His kin are still in the area. A John McLucas was asked to come up with a name for the community when a post office was about to be established, and he chose "Inman."

However, when the railroad was laid down in the late 1880s, there was a train depot on the eastern side of Atlanta called "Inman Yards," Since two Inman depots would be confusing, the train station only in our Inman was called Ackert. No one knows how this name came about.

With the advent of the railroad passing through town in the late 1880s, the commercial district grew to more stores, a gin, and a blacksmith shop.

The town was incorporated in 1911 and it is believed the first mayor was John Ambrose Burch, Sr., Ben Pierce, the blacksmith, was named marshal. There was a small "calaboose" made of 2 x 4's used to incarcerate the rowdy.

When the local school was consolidated with the one in Fayetteville in 1921 the town remained technically incorporated. However, in 1971 it was noted that the county zoning laws applied only in the unincorporated areas and without an active government, all the land lots in Inman were without any zoning protection. So in March of that year, a citizens meeting was held and it was decided to give up the charter.

The area just north of the present Fayetteville city limits is the community of Kenwood.

This is another community from the mid-to late 1880s that we do not know where the name came from. Prior to this name, it was called Davis Crossings, Blalock Station, and Earnest, in honor of a small child who had died, and in 1893 received the name Kenwood.

It was, of course, a lively little business center with stores, a gin house, blacksmith shop, a grist mill, post office, railway station and a dairy.

It was here that the railroad first entered into Fayette County from Atlanta. The train depot is still there.

Kenwood sits in the Europe Militia District. It is suggested it got its name because in bad weather Kenwood's citizens couldn't get out to vote. A new voting place was created here, but a man running in the Blalock district only received one vote in the new district. Apparently disgusted, he made the comment that he didn't want to represent Europe (Kenwood) anyway. Oh well…

In this same area, we have the community of Friendship. It sits at the corner of Highway 314 and Highway 279.

The Friendship United Methodist Church sits at the center of this old community.

The most famous native to come from this area was famed baseball player, Cecil Travis. He was a professional baseball player with the Washington Senators in the 1930s and played in three All Star Games.

The area at Friendship has what might be called a community within a community, Helmer. Its history is parallel to Kenwood and Friendship. It shared the railroad, which brought in business it would not otherwise have gotten.

James H. Helmer owned the dairy and he used the railroad to get his dairy products into Atlanta.

The economy of the Kenwood, Friendship, and Helmer communities continued to prosper until the early 1920s when the boll weevil came in and desecrated our cotton crops.

Land owners throughout our county could hardly make a living on their land, and the sharecroppers had to move to bigger, industrial towns in order to make a living.

Heading back down Highway 92 South, almost to the Spalding county line, we come to the community of Lowry.

It sits by the Flint River and was also on the railroad tracks coming down from Atlanta through Kenwood, Fayetteville, Inman, and Woolsey. Again, these tracks were taken up in 1939.

Lowry no longer has a gin, or grist mill or a sawmill, or a post office, but there are several stores and a gas station.

Sandy Creek community is at the other end of Highway 92, on your way to Fairburn. It also nestles near the communities of Fife, Bethany and Tyrone.

Nearby and close to Tyrone, was the community of Stop. It has been suggested that it got its name from the fact the mail was brought from the Fairburn post office, first by a man walking with a knapsack on his back for six miles. At the end of the six miles someone else would take over and continued for another six miles. When it reached this area the procedure was stopped and the mail went no further.

Mail delivery later came by horse and buggy and delivery was expanded from once a week to three times a week.

The famous Lee's Mill, formerly known in the 1800s as Favor's Mill, sits in this community on Whitewater Creek.

In the 1800s it was a farming community and in the mid-1900s the area around the lake and creek was a popular summer vacation destination for folks coming down from Atlanta. Many owned their own cottage on the lake.

The community of The Rock sits nearby and shares Sandy Creek's heritage. The Rock Church at Sandy Creek Road and Highway 74 north is at this community.

One cannot tell about the various communities in Fayette County without mentioning Gypsy Woods, inhabited when they would be passing through here each year.

Located just south of Woolsey, there were about 20 acres or so given this name. The area was full of chestnut trees and the transients enjoyed camping here. Sometimes they would stay for weeks, the men trading horses and mules and the women homemade goods such as embroidery. They would trade for fresh vegetables, butter, milk and eggs from the local farmers.

The gypsies would also set up "store" on the courthouse square in Fayetteville and this writer would have liked to have seen that sight.

They stopped passing through about the late 1920s.

INCORPORATED
TOWNS—CITIES

Brooks is a community dating back to the county's founding in 1821. It was first called Haistentown. It had a bank in 1910, and was later Hubert Langford's grocery store for 46 years.

BROOKS

The town of Brooks was first settled by "Aunt" Peggy Haisten about 1810 or so. What

The Town of Brooks is a viable one
with wooden buildings replaced by
ones made of brick. This scene is in
the 1940s.

prompted this family to move to an area inhabited only by Indians is a puzzle. However, each seemed to get along with the other and her descendants are still in the area.

In 1821 the first families to legally settle the area had the names of Mills, Washington, Ogden, Glass, Westmoreland, Hardy, Cobb, Moody, Lynch, Pollard, and Kelley. Their descendants still reside in the area.

Two of the early Westmorelands need to be mentioned: Dr. John G. Westmoreland and Dr. Willis Westmoreland.

Dr. John received his primary education at the Fayetteville Academy and his medical education at State Medical College and the Medical College of Philadelphia. He was founder and organizer of Atlanta Medical College, later known as the Atlanta College of Physicians and Surgeons on the campus of what is now Emory University. He was dean at the college for over 40 years.

Dr. William established the *Atlanta Medical and Surgical Journal*. In the War Between The States he established the first hospital at Emory and was an authority on yellow fever long before others in the South.

Brooks is located just two miles west of the Flint River and was located in the Captain Davis District.

It first had the community name of Haistentown in the 1830s, then Sharon Grove, and in 1871 Hillary Brooks sold a lot to the Savannah Griffin and North Alabama Railroad. He asked that in exchange for this consideration that the town would erect a depot on the lot and call the name of the station Brooks.

The town enjoyed a buggy and wagon shop, a shoe shop, a tannery, a general store, and a post office. Until this post office was established in 1871, the nearest post office was in Whitewater.

Brooks was first incorporated in 1910 with a radius of one-half mile. The town charter became inactive about 1922 and in 1964 it was reactivated.

In 1967 an FHA loan was obtained and a water system was put into place. A town hall was built for the mayor and clerk's office. It is now called Hardy Hall. The town bought the former Brooks United Methodist Church when it moved to a new location, and its meetings are held there. It is located adjacent to Hardy Hall. Its current population is 575 persons.

FAYETTEVILLE

See "A County Seat is Created".

PEACHTREE CITY

In the late 1950s a new way of building homes came in to view. It was by making prefabricated concrete slabs and fastening them together.

Pete Knox, II, was in the construction business in the Augusta area. He needed to find an area in which to create a small town in which to build this type of housing. They engaged two real estate men in Atlanta, named Golden and Pickett to locate some 15,000 acres mostly devoid of structures.

They walked into the bank/fertilizer store in Tyrone where Floy Farr was manager and explained their mission. Of course he thought this was an idea that wouldn't last long and suggested they motor down the road to the Aberdeen/Shakerag area on the western side of Fayette County. Since "Mr. Bob" Huddleston owned just over 5,000 acres in that area, he might be persuaded to sell of few of them. He did and received $54 an acre for the first few acres.

When it became obvious that the project might last longer than originally thought, Knox and Farr formed a company. Knox suggested that they needed to acquire over $330,000 to

Peachtree City is celebrating its 50th birthday this spring. This fountain is located in front of its library and city hall.

proceed with the project and this sum was pledged to back it.

Knox had a son who was a senior at Georgia Tech and the son's roommate was Joel Cowan, from Cartersville. Cowan was majoring in Industrial Management and was hired to come up with the plan for a new town and to oversee the whole project.

He not only came up with a viable plan, he also made it work. Fifty years later, it is still working.

Knox began to realize this project was going to require more capital than he could muster, and Cowan found the necessary funds.

Cowan laid out a comprehensive plan for the new town and upon examining this 1959 plan, you will see that it has changed very little in scope. The fascinating part of this plan is that there is no "downtown" Peachtree City. It is laid out in villages with each village having its own shopping facilities.

The Georgia Legislature stated that to create a new town, the town had to have a mayor, and the mayor had to live in the town. Local builder, Huie Bray, was tapped to build a house in the spring of 1959 in 30 days. Cowan became mayor, selected several of the 700 longtime citizens living here to be councilmen, and submitted the project to the legislature. It was approved and Peachtree City became a viable, legal entity.

The first people to move to the new town and to build a brand new house, were the late Jim and Miriam Fulton. However, because the

financial institution in Atlanta felt this project was going to be very short lived, it would only lend them $12,000.

Joel Cowan and the development company had a plan and most importantly they stuck to the plan. By allowing only a certain percentage of the undeveloped land to be sold each year, whether the economic times were good or bad, the town grew in a controlled and stable fashion.

Consequently as Peachtree City celebrates its 50th birthday in March, 2009. The town is almost completely built out and its 36,000 citizens are very proud to live in it.

TYRONE

The town of Tyrone was officially incorporated in 1911 after the Atlanta, Birmingham and Atlantic Railroad was built.

Of course its commercial area grew and a post office was added. Its name was taken from a county in Ireland, which is laid to several reasons: a number of Irish lived in the area, plus the workers laying down the railroad were Irish.

The area has been an agricultural one since the county was established in 1821 but did not have a particular community name.

In the 1800s the main cash crops were cotton and corn, with wheat, oats, ribbon cane, sorghum cane, and sweet potatoes also providing food for families as well as a source of income.

The original settlers built log cabins for their homes. Several remain but have been remodeled and enlarged.

Some of the names of the early settlers are Adams, Callaway, Tinsley, Bearden, Collier, Farr, Handley, Harris, Landrum, Slaton, Stinchcomb and McElwaney.

The first bank in the city was organized in 1907, and purchased by the Redwine brothers in 1912. This bank was moved to Peachtree City just after it was incorporated and became known as the Fayette State Bank.

A hotel was built in 1910 and is now a private residence.

When it was incorporated it contained just over 100 citizens. It has grown to over 7,000 citizens.

Divided by a major state highway, it has also become a major shopping destination with 385 commercial businesses within its city limits.

It is thought that one Thomas Bolling Gay originally owned land on Highway 92 South and he seems to have purchased it from its original land lottery drawer, Jonathan Walker.

He built a home on this land in 1824 and it is still standing. It is known as the Gay-Woolsey-Bell house.

The usual community businesses were in place in the mid 1800s, a grist mill, a blacksmith, and several stores.

Dr. Isaac Gray Woolsey came to the area from Tennessee in 1869. Injured in the War Between The States, he came to Locust Grove, Henry County, and practiced until 1875, at which time he moved to Fayette County.

He purchased the 1824 Gay house and his family would often use the home to accommodate travelers. The area became known

B. E. McElwaney, far left, stands by his store in Tyrone in the 1920s. He served as one of its first councilmen when the town was created in 1911.

❖

Above: The last living teacher at the all black school, built in 1953, is Rosa Penson Anderson. She had been named 1976 Teacher of the Year in the integrated schools.

Below: The Fayette County High School was burned in 1954. It sat where the present Board of Education building is, beside the cemetery.

as "Woolseyville" about the early 1880s and in 1889 it became known as Woolsey.

Woolsey gave land for a school and a cemetery, and he was buried in this cemetery in 1902.

Besides being a doctor he was also an ordained Baptist minister and also served Woolsey in that capacity.

Though there was a mayor and council in the 1800s, that entity became inactive. In 1934 several of the ladies decided the town needed cleaning up and they instituted what might be

called a "petticoat government." The mayor and council consisted of all females and the town was cleaned up, a small park was created and flowers planted.

In the 1920s and 1930s there were hundreds of acres planted behind the Gay-Woolsey-Bell house containing peaches and watermelons. With the train tracks running right through the town, it was a thriving business for a number of years.

Woolsey again instituted a mayor and council in 1972 and those positions are still active today. Its current population is 245 people.

SCHOOLING IN THE COUNTY

As is the case with the white schools, black schools were housed in churches or lodge halls.

In 1955 a comprehensive school was built in Fayetteville for grades one through twelve. It was named The Fayette County Training School. In 1969 the county integrated its schools and it first became the Fayette County Junior High School and then East Fayette Elementary School.

The building's use as a schoolhouse was discontinued in June 2008 and students entered the newly built Inman Elementary School in August 2008. It is the oldest school building in the county.

The only teacher of the original school still living is Rosa Penson Anderson. She was named "Teacher of the Year" in 1976 and was teaching at Peachtree City Elementary School at the time.

The church served as the place for entertainment and simple enjoyment could be found in cake cuttings, box suppers, Christmas activities, and all-night singings.

In school parents were entertained by P. T. A. activities such as plays, dances, talent shows, and spelling bees.

Until the 1920s as many as 21 different schools were scattered throughout the county, for both black and white students.

There were a few school buildings but often classes were held in churches or lodge halls.

Students had to pay a yearly fee to attend these schools.

Some of the schools we have records of include:

In Brooks, it is believed that the first school of record was established between 1850–1860. The first actual school building was erected in the 1880s and was a two-room frame structure.

In 1915 this building burned, and school was held in an empty store building for one term, and in White Water Baptist Church for one term. School buses weren't in the picture yet, so the students had to take their lunch and walk three miles each way to school at White Water.

A school bond issue in Fayette County in 1917 provided funds to build a brick school. In 1920 some of the graduates were Kathryn Crawford (Langford) who returned in 1942 as principal and Crawford Hewell who became a county commissioner.

It needs to be noted, however, that even though a school bond could be issued in the various school districts, the citizens within that particular district had to provide the funding.

One of the names of the small schools nearby is the Longino School and the black school was located in the Macedonia Church.

In Aberdeen and Clover, the school system was typical of those around the county, several one and two room schools were located where a need was found. For a number of years no grade classifications were made. The normal progression was for students to study a book and when finished, they moved into another grade.

The names of some of these smaller schools in this area are Oak Grove, Ebenezer Church, Flat Creek Church, Line Creek, and classes were held at the Shakerag Courthouse.

Each school had its own trustees and if an additional room or repair work was needed, the community people did the work.

In Blackrock the first school known was built a half mile southwest of the Morning Creek bridge on what is now Highway 314.

In the 1870s, Charles J. Robinson donated two acres of land on what is now New Hope Road to be used as a school that was, of course,

❖

Before the 1920s, there were several dozen schools in various communities throughout the county. The Robinson School sat on New Hope Road, not far from the New Hope Baptist Church.

The Edgefield Baptist Church sits appropriately on Church Street in Fayetteville. Here Dan Savant, Tourgée Simpson, Larry Clark, and Bruce Walker plan for the future.

to be named for him. It was completed prior to 1880 and used until 1940 when it consolidated with the county and the students then went into Fayetteville.

The community at Flat Creek had a church with a school nearby in the early and mid 1800s. It was a two-room school and in later years it went by the name of Askew and then Union Grove school.

The grades were first thru seventh and it was governed by four trustees. They were elected for their Christian character. If a teacher did not measure up to standards of the community the trustees quietly dismissed them and quietly found another one. Yes, discipline in those years applied to the young and not so young.

While the school no longer remains, the church still does.

The school at Fife was located in the Bethany Methodist Church. No more is known about it.

The school in the Hopeful community of Tyrone consisted of logs with slabs for seats and was located in the south corner of Lee's Mill Road and Georgia Highway 92.

A new school was built in the mid 1880s and was considered quite modern with three rooms and was white paint. It was consolidated in 1951 with the schools in Fayetteville.

A local doctor paid $600 a year for a teacher and the children could attend school here for

$1.00 per month tuition. It was known as the Hopeful Academy.

It is thought that there were no schools in Inman until the state of Georgia established a state school system.

In 1889 the trustees of Inman Academy were paying the principal $500 to teach for eight months. If there was any money left from paying the assistant principal $75 per month, it was to go to the principal on top of his $500.

In 1895 a contract was devised between the trustees of the Inman High School and famed teacher, J. W. Culpepper. He was to be paid $1.50 to $2 per pupil per month, according to grade, and proper reductions being made for public funds.

The Inman school district was incorporated as such in 1901. This district was abolished in 1921 and consolidated with Fayetteville.

There was a black school here near the New Hope A.M.E. Church. It was closed in 1955 when the Fayette Training School was built in Fayetteville. The church, however, is still a viable one.

The first teacher known in the school at Friendship was Omar Lee. He taught at the local schools at Friendship, Rest, Hopeful, Bethsaida and Blackrock. It is said he was the last teacher here before he left for World War I.

Sandy Creek had a school in the Sandy Creek Baptist Church until one could be built in 1905. Several years later, this building burned and everyone had to attend school some two miles away, at The Rock School.

After that school was held in several buildings near the burned-out one. The second schoolhouse built was built about 1910 and in the 1940s it was consolidated with Fayetteville.

The area around Tyrone contained several different schools, going by the names of Rocky Mount, Hopewell Academy, Swanson School, Askew School, Little Vine, and Flat Rock School.

Rocky Mount was a one-room building on Farr Road.

Hopewell Academy was founded in 1849 and it was a 30 x 20 foot building and was built by subscriptions of $67.50. Boys were seated on one side and girls on the other. Heat was from two fireplaces. It was just east of the former site of the Hopewell United Methodist Church. In 1929 it was consolidated with Fayetteville.

The Swanson School was a one-room log building with a large fireplace. It was located on Old Senoia Road. It was later remodeled to be a home.

The Askew School was one of the last schools to be used after consolidation. It sat at Tyrone Road and Flat Creek Trail. It contained long benches and double-wide school desks. It was later rebuilt and renamed Union Grove School and had two rooms with a center hall.

Little Vine and Flat Rock schools were used as both schools and churches. Little Vine is located in the community of Stop. The Little Vine Baptist Church and the Flat Rock Church are still viable.

In the community of Woolsey Dr. I. G. Woolsey gave the land for the first school house. A two-story building was erected with the first floor to be the school. It had a stage on one end. The second floor was to be used as both a Masonic Lodge and the Woodmen Lodge, and some school activities.

A new brick building was built in 1929 for the sum of $10,000. It consisted of four classrooms, an auditorium, and rooms on either side that were later converted into restrooms.

Mount Springs was a school nearby that eventually consolidated with Woolsey.

CHURCHES

We are only going to discuss those churches whose beginnings were in the 1800s.

From 1826 to 1829, there were five churches duly constituted in Fayette County, and every one is still a viable congregation.

All in all, there were about 24 viable congregations in the 1800s, and by and large, they are still open and doing the Lord's business.

In contrast, in 2008, there are just over 100 "churches", with 80 of them having their own permanent sanctuary. The others are "store front" churches.

Let's talk about those first five churches constituted just after our county was created in 1821. Four are Baptist churches and one is a Methodist church.

The Fayetteville First United Methodist Church has been located in several different areas around the present site. The current site has been in existence since about 1900. The church was constituted in 1825. The circuit preacher served the area that might include as many as six other counties. The most he might be paid is $180 a year by each church. At first each church might only be able to have one service a month and it was not until the late 1880s that this increased to two services a month. With the main Methodist and main Baptist churches directly across the street from one another, it was not unusual for both

The Fayetteville First United Methodist Church is one of the five created in the 1820s and is still viable. This one sat on the current site about 1900.

congregations to visit whichever church had a circuit preacher on that Sunday. In 1937 this congregation was named as a full station, and it was able to hire and have its very own preacher. At this time a new facility was built and serves as its Chapel for smaller occasions. The three-story education building was built in 1957 and it contains a new sanctuary, built in 1987, and Family Life Center, built in 1998. It has about 1,900 members on its roll.

The Fayettevile First Baptist Church was begun in 1828 with the name Shiloh Baptist Church. However, it sat five miles out of Fayetteville near the present Redwine Road. It began with the leadership of White Water Baptist. Land was donated by William Bennett and when the church moved to Fayetteville in 1842, it reverted back to the Bennett estate. One and a half acres were purchased at its present site for $75. It still retained the name of Shiloh until 1851 when it was changed to Baptist Church of Christ at Fayetteville, and in 1854 it became Fayetteville Baptist Church. Its latest addition was built in 2003. It currently has over 1,600 members.

The Antioch Baptist Church was constituted in 1829 and is located near Woolsey. The first Sunday School was put in place in 1845 with 56 pupils. In 1850 it was decided to build a new facility that would be 40 x 60 feet. It was completed in 1851. Land was purchased to contain the church and a cemetery in 1892. This land was purchased for just over $35 per acre for 5 and a half acres. It was declared able to have a full-time pastor in 1965. The first preacher in 1829 was Robert Stell, whose family descendants are still living in the county. It is privileged to have all of its original church minutes from the beginning. There are currently 70 members in the church.

The White Water Baptist Church served as the Mother Church to others in the county and general area. The first church sat west of the present one which is located on 85 Connector. It was used in 1971 as a part of the county's sesquicentennial. A dinner on the grounds was held with everyone in "old-timey" costumes. The church enjoys a current membership of 79 persons.

The Flat Creek Baptist Church is located on Flat Creek Trail with its cemetery across the road as well as behind it. It was constituted in August 1826, under the leadership of White Water Baptist. The first building was erected in 1827 about a quarter of a mile west of its current site. In 1874, a new meeting house was voted on and it was to be a 40 x 60 structure. It was dedicated in March 1876. The cost was about $695. In 1907 it was voted to buy three acres at $10 an acre where the current facility is located. While the present building was built in 1957 it has been greatly added to and remodeled. In the early days there was no church treasurer, so a collection would be take up for such needs as oil for lamps, paying to clean out the well, or to pay the preacher. It is noted that in 1845 all members were required to pay 25 cents to defray church expenses.

It is interesting to note that while they all started under brush arbors, then went from a log cabin facility to white wooden buildings, today these five physical plants are worth more than $20 million dollars.

OTHER VIABLE CHURCHES BEGUN IN THE 1800s

County Line Christian Church is thought to have begun in the late 1820s in Brooks and met at a doctor's shop. In 1845, it obtained its own building. It was the second Christian Church to be organized in Georgia.

The Hopeful Primitive Baptist Church is believed to have also begun in the 1820s. It is located at the corner of New Hope Road and N. Highway 92. It now has just a couple of members.

The Hopewell United Methodist Church was begun in Tyrone in 1849 and its original name was Hopewell Methodist Protestant Church.

Rowland Stubbs deeded an acre and a half in 1849 for a meeting house in Inman, and Liberty Chapel was built. It is now Inman United Methodist Church.

Flat Rock A.M.E. church is the oldest African-American church in the county. It dates

Opposite page, top: The Fayetteville Methodist chapel was built in 1937 under the leadership of Hill P. Redwine. His niece, Henrietta, married Doug Dennis and they were the first couple married in it. It is still in use.

Opposite page, bottom: The Fayetteville First Baptist Church is one of the five churches created in the 1820s that is still a viable congregation. Shown here is the Overton Chapel.

Below: Flat Creek Baptist Church is one of the five churches created in the 1820s that is still a viable congregation. Shown here are members during a baptism in 1914 at Lake Bennett.

FLAT CREEK CHURCH, LAKE BENNETT: 1914

County Line Christian Church dates back to the early 1800s. It sits at the corners of Fayette, Coweta, and Spalding Counties.

to 1854 and is located just behind the post office building on Highway 54, halfway between Fayetteville and Peachtree City. It has a historical plaque in front in conjunction with the Fayette County Historical Society.

Bethany United Methodist Church is located at the corner of Lee's Lake Road and Rivers Road in the northern part of the county. The congregation began in 1856. It is famous for its Perlieu Stew, held each Fall.

Brooks United Methodist Church began about 1861. The church built in 1902 now serves as the Brooks Town Hall and the new facility is at 119 Morgan Mill Road.

Bethlehem Baptist Church was organized in 1866. It is located at 475 Dividend Drive, Peachtree City. It is one of two churches with an historic plaque in front erected in conjunction with the Georgia Historical Society.

Flint Ridge Baptist Church was organized in 1866 and is located at 101 Old Ridge Road in north Fayetteville.

Mt. Olive Baptist Church was organized in 1867. In the spring of 2008 it built a new facility at 1565 N. Highway 92.

Edgefield Baptist Church began in 1870 at a big granite rock at the corner of Hickory Avenue and Highway 54 in Fayetteville. It is currently located at 140 Church Street, Fayetteville.

New Hope United Methodist is at 618 Inman Road in Inman. The congregation goes back to the late 1870s.

Merrill Chapel United Methodist has a congregation going back to 1877 and is located at 435 S. Jeff Davis Drive, Fayetteville.

Macedonia Baptist Church was organized in 1880 and was located on McIntosh Road in Brooks. It remained active until about the year 2000.

Hartford United Methodist Church can be found at 202 Padgett Road in south Fayette County. It was founded about 1880.

Lisbon Baptist Church was organized in 1880 by members of Antioch Baptist Church. It is located at 1662 S. Highway 82.

The New Hope Baptist Church was begun in 1880 in a small white church building and the congregation now has a membership of nearly 6,000 worshipers. It is located at 551 New Hope Road. The original building has been preserved on the site.

The worshipers at Ebenezer United Methodist Church have been doing so since the 1880s. It is located in the middle of the county at 680 Ebenezer Road.

In 1882 the Sandy Creek Baptist Church was established. It is at the junction of Sandy Creek Road and Jenkins Road. Its original name was

Church of Christ at Sandy Creek, and in 1939 it acquired its present name.

Little Vine Baptist Church is located at 115 Handley Road in Tyrone. It was organized in 1888. The church also served as a school.

Glen Grove Baptist Church began in 1887 at Starr's Mill. It has since become a part of New Hope Baptist Church South.

Woolsey Baptist Church was first constituted in 1888 as the Harmony Grove Baptist Church. It was given the present name in 1904. One of the first elders and pastors was Dr. I. G. Woolsey.

Friendship United Methodist Church sits at the corner of Highway 314 and Highway 279. The congregation dates back to 1890.

Holly Grove A.M.E. began in 1897 in south Fayette County and is technically now located in Peachtree City. It is one of two churches in the county with an historic plaque that was erected in conjunction with the Georgia Historical Society.

Please let us know if we have accidentally omitted any of these valuable assets to our community.

Information was taken from *The History of Fayette County*, published in 1977 and oral interviews by the author with various citizens, including Joe Morton, City Manager, The City of Fayetteville; and Craig Gross, Extension Agent, Fayette County.

New Hope Baptist Church began in the 1880s and is still located on the same site. The building shown here has been preserved. This photo dates about 1940.

Top: This mural depicting various scenes around the county faces south. The principal artists were Ed and Patsy Gullett.

Center: Both Fayetteville and the Fayette County administration get together to decorate for the Christmas season.

Bottom: In 1986 the Margaret Mitchell-Fayette County Public Library moved to new quarters. Over 13,000 books were moved by hand to the new site in 4 hours. Since 1988 the building has housed the Fayette County Historical Society.

Above: In 1976 the National Bicentennial Wagon Train came through Fayette County and spent the night. It was housed at the stables that existed at that time in Peachtree City. From left: Frank Rickman, Georgia Wagonmaster, Carolyn Cary, Fayette County chairman, and Harry Lee, National Wagonmaster.

Below: This mural is one of two painted on businesses in downtown Fayetteville. Local artist Andy Billingsley painted this one. Coca-Cola approved the design.

PAINTING BY VICKI TURNER.

SHARING THE HERITAGE

Historic profiles of businesses,

organizations, and families that have

contributed to the development and

economic base of Fayette County

SPECIAL THANKS TO

Aunt Laura's Sweet
Shoppe & Tea Room

PEACHTREE LAW GROUP

Peachtree Law Group, a legal mainstay in the history of Fayette County and the metro area since the early 1980s, continues to emphasize integrity, honesty, respect and professionalism in providing comprehensive, varied services to its many clients.

"Our firm stays on the cutting edge of technology by utilizing the most advanced tools in representing clients and litigating cases," said David R. Moore, founder of the firm. "We have a goal and commitment to provide the same quality of legal care for each case and to treat each client as a member of our family."

The foundation for the firm was laid when Moore, now managing and senior partner of the Law Group, graduated Atlanta Law School and began the practice of law in 1984. In 1989 he founded Melnick, Moore and Elliott where he was managing partner. Four of the five partners from the firm formed Peachtree Law Group in 1999 and added lawyers who specialize in a wide spectrum of the law.

The background and experience of the firm's five partners and two associates are indicative of the same excellent representation that the Moore group has provided clients since 1984.

Moore has a long, varied and distinguished career in the law, legal field and civic and community affairs. He is a retired Atlanta police officer, where he earned Officer of the Year, Public Safety Employee of the Year and the

Mayoral Award. For twelve years, he gained invaluable experience deciding cases in Fulton State Court and Fulton Superior Court as an Arbiter. His many professional and civic activities include President and life member of the South Fulton Bar Association, president of the Fayette Bar Association, and editor of Christian books. Active in Rotary, he has served on the board of Peachtree City Rotary, attorney for the club, chaired its International Service Committee, and served on the Rotary International Annual Conference Committee and Membership Development Committee, among others. Moore also has served on the Fayette Chamber Board, its Governmental Affairs Committee, Legislative Committee and Chairman's Roundtable. He has been very active on the Advisory Board of Fayette County United Way, chairing the Financial Investment Committee and serving on the campaign committee.

The firm's mission statement, "To glorify God by being a faithful steward of all that is entrusted to us and to have a positive influence on all who come in contact with Peachtree Law Group," reflects Moore's religious commitment. He enjoys mission work and teaching children's Sunday School at New Hope Church in Fayetteville.

During Moore's year as President of the Fayette Bar Association, the membership doubled. This year was the only year in its history the growth was one hundred percent. Moore led many committees and was first to the call. On just one occasion, he went under the Fayette Samaritan house in the mud to secure the floor joist as one of his jobs, not to mention the shoveling of dirt for hours. Superior Court Judge Tommy Hankinson and other Fayette lawyers participated and the event was a great success. Superior Court Judges Chris Edwards and Johnnie Caldwell, Jr., and State Court Judge Fletcher Sams have always been instrumental in giving valuable advice to the Fayette Bar Association.

The work by Moore in United Way took him to work with the Fayette Youth Protection Home, Johnson Home and others. While he chaired the Financial Investment Committee, he visited many locations funded by United Way and influenced the rapport with them for a better community.

Other members of the Law Group are partners Larry M. Melnick, David J. Couch, J. Michael Brennan, and James C. Brown. Serving of counsel to the firm are Kenneth H. Green and Clifford W. Milam.

- Melnick served twelve years on the State Bar of Georgia Board of Governors. He was President of the Clayton County Bar Association and a Fellow of the Lawyers Foundation of Georgia. He is the recipient of the Clayton County Lifetime Achievement Award, State Bar Tradition in Excellence Award and the American Jurisprudence Award.

- Couch, a native of East Point, is a 1972 graduate of Atlanta's Russell High School and earned undergraduate accounting, master of taxation and law degrees from Georgia State University. He is a certified public accountant who practiced with local and international firms prior to entering the legal profession and joining the Law Group. He is a fellow of the Lawyers Foundation of Georgia and Georgia Institute of Certified Public Accountants.

- Brennan is a native of Cincinnati and earned a BA in political science from the University of Florida in 1996 and a Doctor of Jurisprudence from Western New England College School of Law in 2000. He is a member of the Real Estate Law Section of the State Bar of Georgia.

- Brown, a native of Atlanta, graduated from Murphy High School in 1956 and then served three years in the Army. He is a graduate of Georgia State in 1973 with a BS degree and earned his law degree from Atlanta Law School five years later. He has practiced law since 1978 and his areas of expertise include

❖

The staff of Peachtree Law Group.
Front: James C. Brown, David R.
Moore, and Michael J. Brennan.
Center: Mary Kachman, Annette
Forlines, Catherine Stevens, Fawn
Moore, and Pam Moore.
Back: David J. Couch, Ben Parks
(Investigator), Kenneth H. Green,
Larry M. Melnick and
Clifford W. Milam.

personal injury and general litigation. Currently he is enjoying being semi-retired, working from his lake home in north Georgia.

- Green, also a native Atlantan, graduated from the city's Brown High School, like Moore, he in 1968 and Moore in 1971. Green did undergraduate work at Clayton State College and Georgia State University. Also, like Moore, he is retired from the Atlanta Police Department, where he rose to the rank of major. In 1998, Green was the recipient of the Atlanta Bar Association's Liberty Bell Award. He graduated from Atlanta Law School in 1980 and has practiced law in the metro area since that time. He is also a staff attorney for neighboring Clayton County.
- Milam was born in Red Oak, Georgia, in 1922. He graduated from Campbell High School in 1940 and his undergraduate work was done at Georgia State University. He then enlisted in the US Air Force for five years. He worked for Delta Airlines and Prudential Insurance before graduating from Atlanta Law School. He began his law practice in 1950 and has practiced in the Atlanta area for fifty plus years. Milam is enjoying retirement.

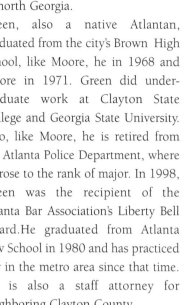

Former prominent attorneys from PLG include Christy Dunkelburger who is now a founding partner in the firm of Pierce and Dunkelburger in Fayetteville. Mary Lynn Kirby and John Nix are founding partners in the firm of Kirby, Palmer, Farrell and Nix, also known as Fayette Law Group in Fayetteville.

Moore's wife, Pam, is the Office Manager and Senior Legal Assistant for the firm. His oldest

Above: Moore with Randall Johnson, who has been Sheriff of Fayette County for thirty-two years and is a fellow church member.

Below: Presentation was made by Fayette Bar President David Moore to Superior Court Chief Judge Paschal English, and Commission Chairman Greg Dunn (pictured with Moore). Magistrate Judge Bob Rupenthal and Superior Court Judge Chris Edwards, along with David Moore, facilitated the acquisition and presentation of the plaque.

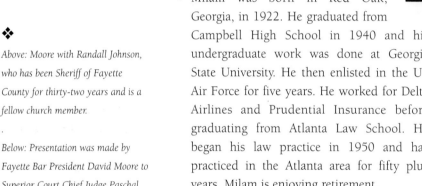

child, Reba Dever, is a Senior Legal Assistant in a north Atlanta firm. His twenty-one year old daughter, Fawn Moore, works at PLG, is completing her Bachelor degree at the University of Georgia, and is planning to attend law school.

David's father, Walter Milner Moore, handed David a slip of paper the minute after he was sworn in as an attorney (1984), which had his first client's name printed. David won that jury trial in Judge Andrew Whalen's court and has had a successful practice ever since. David's first appearance (non-jury) in court was in front of Judge Ben Miller in Fayette County, at the

little strip building (Annex) behind the Waffle House restaurant on Georgia Highway 85 in Fayetteville. Moore's practice includes professional negligence, focusing on Legal Malpractice, where he sues lawyers.

Moore is a Sustaining Life Fellow of the Lawyer's Foundation of Georgia. The invitation to membership in the Fellows Program is an honor that recognizes those lawyers whose public and private careers demonstrate outstanding legal abilities and a devotion to their communities and the highest standards of the profession. This honor is limited to three percent of the trial lawyers in the State.

Above: The conference room and inside office of Peachtree Law Group.

Below: The Peachtree Law Group is located at 125 Flat Creek Trail, in Fayetteville, and at www.peachtreelawgroup.com.

AUTREY'S ARMORY, INC.

❖

Above: Autrey's Armory,
Inc., storefront.

PHOTO COURTESY OF BEN AUTREY.

Below: Retail area with shotguns,
rifles, and handguns.

PHOTO COURTESY OF BEN AUTREY.

Founded in 2003, Autrey's Armory, Inc., has quickly gained a reputation for being the place to be for metro Atlanta's gun enthusiasts. Autrey's Armory offers a complete range of firearms services, including Fayette County's first public indoor shooting range. The Armory's success can be measured by a twenty percent increase in gross sales annually since its opening

five years ago, an above average figure for a business of its kind.

"We have been fortunate to have a steady, dedicated clientele from throughout the metro area," owner Ben Autrey commented.

Being in business to serve gun owners and aficionados comes naturally to Autrey, who has been a gun enthusiast since his childhood in Enterprise, Alabama. Autrey attended Auburn University where he was an active member of ROTC and a 1996 Building Science graduate.

Autrey, commissioned as a Second Lieutenant in the Third Infantry Division, served as a platoon leader in support, scout, and combat engineer platoons. When he left active duty in 1999 he relocated to Fayetteville and worked as an assistant project manager for Leslie Contracting, Inc. Later, his interest in guns led him to a job at a local gun store, Adventure Arms, LTD. He was the store's manager for three years before deciding to open his own store. In addition to owning Autrey's Armory, he stays busy with community involvement and with his family: wife, Sheila, and daughters, Lauren and Emma.

Opening a gun store and indoor shooting range is not an easy task. Thanks to Dustin Uselton, Milton McKnight and Amos Grimes, key players in starting and keeping the business going, Autrey's continues to grow. Currently, a complement of seventeen employees, well-versed in all things guns, helps carry out the Armory's mission to offer comprehensive firearms services.

The Armory's twenty-five yard indoor shooting range holds twelve lanes where customers can practice firing personal or store-rented guns.

"Our state-of-the-art indoor shooting range features two bays with six lanes each. All twelve lanes are a full twenty-five yards in length. Our rifle bay can handle all rifle calibers up to and including .300 Win Mag. The range equipment is manufactured by Caswell Detroit Armor and uses a new technology to virtually eliminate the chance of ricochets and lead dust. The ventilation and lighting systems are well thought out to provide a safe and enjoyable shooting environment," Autrey elaborated.

The retail side of the Armory offers customers a wide array of brands that gun enthusiasts are sure to recognize, including Glock, Smith & Wesson, Kimber, Browning, Springfield, Ruger, Les Baer, Ed Brown, CZ, Rock River Arms, Beretta, Remington, Benelli, Leupold, Nighforce, Swarovski, Trijicon, SureFire, Galco, Benchmade, Advanced Armament, Gemtech, Tactical Solutions and many others.

Additional conveniences for the Armory's customers include various firearms training classes, Class 3 sales and transfers, and an on-site gunsmith.

"We offer daily and annual memberships and host a variety of leagues and competitions. Handgun rentals are also available," he added.

Recently Autrey's Armory gained national attention when it appeared in segments on NBC's *The Today Show* and Food Network's *Good Eats*, whose host is metro Atlanta's Alton Brown.

Autrey's Armory is dedicated to local civic and community affairs, sponsoring many activities including those with Rotary Clubs, 4-H Clubs and the Joseph Sams School. Its charitable

contributions have also gone to various police, sheriff and fire department fundraisers.

Autrey's Armory, Inc., is located in the Lee Center off Highway 314, at 116 Bethea Road, Suite 118 in Fayetteville and on the Internet at www.AutreysArmory.com.

❖

Above: Handgun Safety Class with Pat Sennett, instructor, and students Don Thompson, Waynette MacFarlane, Art Wolfenson and Gayle Wolfenson.

PHOTO COURTESY OF BEN AUTREY.

Left: Indoor rifle and pistol ranges.

PHOTO COURTESY OF BEN AUTREY.

WALKER CONCRETE

In 1953, Barney Walker, Georgia Huddleston, Willie Huddleston, and Crawford Bailey put up $2,000 each and opened a small company, Farmers and Builders Supply. Later the supply part of the business was sold and the name was changed to Fayette Concrete. Over the next several decades that modest operation evolved into Walker Concrete, which has been instrumental in helping build some of the area's most important institutional and commercial structures.

During its long and storied history the company has been a family affair with the extended Walker family, including sons, daughters, sons-in-law, and grandchildren, all contributing to its successful operation.

The company's first big job was pouring concrete for the Fayette Training School, now the East Fayette School, which required a modest three hundred yards of cement, which had to be opened by hand and poured into a mixer. A year later the company began its modernization when it bought a mixer to mount on the back of its truck.

In 1960 the firm opened Clayton Concrete Company in Jonesboro, which poured all of the massive amounts of cement for an Atlanta landmark, the Atlanta International Raceway. It was a time when concrete was just $12.25 a yard and the company used $50,000 worth of cement a month on the job.

In 1967, Clayton Concrete poured the concrete for two of Clayton County's most important institutions: Clayton General Hospital, now known as Southern Regional Hospital, and Clayton Junior College, which is now a four year school, Clayton State University.

As plants were added the name was changed to Walker Concrete, growing to nine locations and fourteen plants. One big problem was left-over concrete. The company was always looking for places to dump it. Around 1980, Barney had the idea of recycling concrete. It is a drying process. This turned out to be a big savings for the company. This process was approved by the Georgia Department of Transportation for a base on streets and driveways. This process was named the "Barney Run" and is still used today.

Various early redi-mix trucks, Barney and Sue Walker, 1951.

For the past thirty years Doug Walker, the oldest son of parents Sue and Barney, has served as president of the company. After working for Walker Concrete for several years, their youngest son, Dell, founded Walker Brothers Trucking Company as a vehicle to help manage the company's inventory of sand, rock and bulk cement. He expanded the business from stockpiling materials to hauling to job sites, both residential and commercial.

Barney, a native of Fayette County, commented that his fifty years in the business has been a challenging, but enjoyable line of work. "I've looked forward to the job and building a business for my family and community every day."

His parents were members of the Fayetteville First Baptist Church and Barney attended at an early age and is still an active member. He especially likes to welcome members and visitors to services.

Barney got his work ethic from his father, a local farmer and carpenter who taught his sons his craft and the value of hard work. Before entering the concrete business Barney built homes in Fayette County, and he and his brother owned a service station. He also was a substitute mail carrier for several years.

Barney and his wife, the former Sue Hancock, also a Fayette native, have four children—Doug, Dell, Rose, and Jamie—all of whom graduated from Fayette County High School. The couple has twelve grandchildren.

Active in local civic and community affairs for more than five decades, Barney served 8 years on the Fayetteville City Council, 4 years on the County Board of Education, 4 years on the Fayette Planning and Zoning Committee, and 28 years as a director of several local banks.

The company that Barney helped found in 1953 came full circle when it was purchased by National Cement Company of Birmingham, Alabama, in April 2008.

Family affair: Rose, Doug, Jamie, Dell, Sue and Barney.

NEW HOPE BAPTIST CHURCH

Proverbs 29:18 says, "Where there is no vision, the people will perish." A reversal of this truth would be, "Where there is a vision, the people will flourish." This has proven true in the life of New Hope Baptist Church. New Hope has flourished due to the vision instilled by God in the hearts of a faithful few over 128 years ago.

The Baptist Church of Christ at New Hope was established September 1880. The first building, a makeshift one-room structure, was completed in 1883. Reverend J. G. Speights served as the first pastor. A new one-room wood structure was completed in 1901 and remains in use today.

The early church consisted of close knit, hardworking people who shared the burdens of fellow church members and neighbors. That tradition continues today. Each holiday season, New Hope delivers over 250 food baskets and gives Angel gifts to families.

The church "visitation program" began in 1907 with a "move and second that a brother go visit another brother and get him to come to church." In 2008, New Hope members visited 4,500 families.

All-day singings combined with good homemade food were big events for the early church. Today we gather for our annual barbecue and baptism at our South Campus at Starr's Mill.

On June 1, 1926, the name of New Hope Church of Christ at New Hope was shortened to New Hope Baptist Church.

With Reverend Richard Lee as pastor, a new 550-seat facility was completed in 1976. The congregation marched into the new building singing "Standing on the Promises." During this time, New Hope became one of the most vital churches in the area. Upon Reverend Lee's resignation in June 1978, Reverend Dwight "Ike" Reighard was called as pastor.

Church membership quickly increased to 1,200. When asked the secret of New Hope's success, Dr. Reighard responded, "The people of New Hope believe in prayer and witnessing to others." This continues to be the heart of New Hope. In 1985 a 2,100-seat facility was opened. After seventeen years as pastor, Dr. Reighard accepted a pastoral position with a church in the Atlanta area and Dr. John Avant was called to fill the position.

Offering the largest convention facility in Fayette County, New Hope hosts up to five baccalaureate services and two graduations annually, the Fayette County Board of Education New Teacher Orientation Breakfast and Training, the Fayette County Board of Education Coaches' Banquet, the Fayette

County Business Expo, the Upward Sports Program averaging 2,000 weekly, and in partnership with other local churches, a baseball clinic for approximately 1,500 participants.

Annual mission trips are made to seven countries. A ten-year mission partnership with Holland Road Baptist Church, Brighton-Hove England, led to the call of New Hope's current pastor, Reverend Rhys Stenner, former pastor of Holland Road.

Reverend Stenner leads New Hope with an emphasis on families, prayer, and bringing others to the saving knowledge of Jesus Christ. The Living Christmas Tree Program is the most popular program offered to the community and is the largest event held in the county with over ten thousand attending annually. Wednesday night L.I.F.E. (Learn, Invest, Find, Explore) classes include parenting, finances, information technology, scrap-booking, sewing, and the opportunity to go deeper into God's Word. Classes are attended by many non-members.

Members of New Hope established a home for unwed mothers, which is now located at the Georgia Baptist Children's Home in Palmetto, Georgia. We are involved in the Fayette County Youth Protection Program and support the Southwest Christian Hospice and the Real Life Center in Tyrone, which offers benevolence and food assistance. New Hope provides an acre site and supports the "Plant a Row for the Hungry" program, a national program encouraging gardeners to plant additional vegetables to help food banks and kitchens. This year over 22,000 pounds were harvested on this site. New Hope is the recipient of the "Partner in Education" award for the renovation of the playground at North Fayette Elementary School.

"One Church in Two Locations," New Hope provides facilities on the North and South ends of the county. Our membership and growth reflect the rich diversity of our county. A church like New Hope is not an accident. It is the answer to prayers that have spanned 128 years. The vision God placed in the hearts of the founding fathers lives in the hearts of the church body today as we seek to serve and share the love of Jesus Christ with our community, state, nation and world.

REALLY KILLER SYSTEMS

Fayetteville's Really Killer Systems (RKS, Inc.) got its start in 1993 when founder and part owner, Jim Beck, came up with an innovative idea for a product that dramatically simplified the conversion of coin operated games to dispense tickets. With the financial backing of friend Don Baker, he and his wife, Mary, began assembling the new product by hand on their kitchen table. With Don's help in distribution, it became an overnight success.

Now an electronics and development firm whose primary focus is on products for the commercial coin operated market, remote

controlled aircraft and the electronics hobbyist market, RKS has lived up to its name of making "killer products that kill the competition," Jim comments only half in jest.

When the firm introduced its product there were twelve similar ones on the market. Within one year there were only three. Today, RKS dominates the market.

Although the coin-op industry has been the major thrust of the company, it has completed several successful larger game projects. RKS has been involved in projects as diverse as a Dash-CAM systems for law enforcement vehicles and water treatment systems for pork farms. "Our real love is to do R&D for limited run products at a reasonable price. In other words, we like to make widgets and gadgets," Jim enthuses.

What was to become RKS had an inauspicious beginning when Jim's idea was turned down by his boss at the coin operated device distributor for whom he was working. The product, which would eventually replace existing technology that was bulky, expensive and difficult to install, was rejected as too expensive and not in line with the company's business mode. That's when Jim went to his friend, Don, who agreed to help fund the start-up company and be the sole distributor through his company, Home Leisure.

With Jim and Mary producing the product and Don doing the distribution, RKS was off and running. As the product line grew, Home Leisure was merged into the start-up company, now known as RKS, Inc.

Within a few months of operation, RKS was selling units by the thousands and began

outsourcing some of the work. At this time, friends Tony and Shirley Noel volunteered to help as contract manufacturers.

In 1997, RKS moved to its current location at 137 Bethea Road in Fayetteville. The following year, Sandy Butler joined RKS to do technical support and product repairs. In 2000, Don retired, and he and his wife, Sophie, sold their shares to Tony and Shirley.

Today, Jim, Mary, Tony, Shirley and Sandy, are the principals of the company. There are also several local, national and international subcontractors and suppliers.

RKS occasionally has the opportunity to be an active part in the design of a new arcade style game. "When this occurs, our children are brought in to test the game before it is returned to the manufacturer," Jim explained. "The children love this, as they get bragging

rights to having played a game before it is released to the public. The manufacturer also gets the added benefit of having it child tested."

Still a small, self-contained business, RKS now has four full time employees with plans to hire others as the business grows. It is primarily a mail-order operation with a COD payment system which eliminates some overhead expenses.

The company has been profitable from its inception and has continued to grow over the years.

"Our philosophy is, if it isn't broke, don't fix it," Jim emphasized. "But if it does break, tear it down and make it better."

"We are constantly looking for the next big idea that will take us into the future. With this in mind, we will continue to grow and expand our market as needed," he added.

Active in the community, Mary mainly represents RKS in local events and organizations.

RKS is a Fayette County chamber member, a Partner in Education, sponsor of the Sheriff's Boys Home and the NASCAR Children's Charity.

WEBB, LINDSEY & WADE, LLC

When Jim Webb, a partner in a local Peachtree City law firm, and Rick Lindsey, an associate there, decided it was time to start their own firm they pledged it would be one with the needed flexibility, expertise and depth to offer first class representation they believed their clients would need and deserve.

Founded on the first day of 1992, over the nearly two decades it has been in business, Webb, Lindsey & Wade has fulfilled that pledge by building a full service law practice which provides quality expertise in several different key areas of the law.

With emphasis in civil litigation in such diverse fields as medical malpractice and automobile/truck collisions, business transactions and formations, estate planning and wills, probate, adoptions, and local government and zoning laws, the firm's experienced and highly trained staff of attorneys and support groups now has consolidated operations in its original Peachtree City location after having closed offices in Buckhead and Fairburn.

Within two years of its formation, the firm had more than doubled in size. The original office was too small to accommodate the growth of what was then called Webb & Lindsey. Some of the lawyers were working in windowless offices not any bigger than closets and the firm administrator actually worked in the supply closet. There was no choice but to move to a much bigger office, which it did in December of 1995. Within two more years the firm had outgrown its space again and added the Buckhead and Fairburn offices. Webb & Lindsey now boasted eighteen lawyers and an equal number of support staff. While the firm had clearly exploded in growth, the main office always remained in Peachtree City.

Jon Wade, who worked for a law firm in DeKalb County's county seat of Decatur, joined the firm in 1997 and subsequently was named partner. He added to the organization's already strong line-up of legal expertise with several years of both courtroom and classroom experience, having taught law at an Atlanta law school.

The firm's explosive growth and, at the time multiple locations, caused its attorneys to embrace technology before many other business people were aware of the Internet and e-mail. Lawyers in

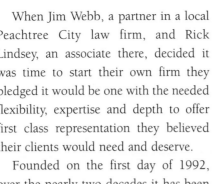

❖

Above: James H. Webb, Jr.

Below: Jonathan J. Wade.

the organization quickly took crash courses in how to master this new way to communicate with clients.

Both of the firm's founders are cum laude graduates of the University of Georgia Law School and are natives of nearby College Park.

After attending Georgia State University and serving in Vietnam as an Army First Lieutenant, Jim received his law doctorate in Athens. Shortly after graduation he moved to Florida and then returned to his home state to set up a law practice in Newnan, while moving his family, wife Debbie and two young daughters, to Peachtree City. Upon becoming City Attorney for Peachtree City, he opened an office and joined forces with other local attorneys until founding what is now Webb, Lindsey & Wade. Jim is a former chairman of the General Practice & Trial Section of the Georgia Bar and has been named a "Georgia Super Lawyer" by *Atlanta Magazine*.

Rick also attended Georgia State where he obtained a Bachelor of Business Administration degree magna cum laude before going to law school in Athens where he not only graduated cum laude, but was a member of the editorial board of the *Georgia Law Review*. Upon graduation Rick went to Birmingham, Alabama, to serve as a law clerk for Federal Judge William T. Acker, Jr., of the United States District Court for the Northern District of Alabama. Following his clerkship, he returned to an Atlanta law firm. In 1987, he and his wife, Cindy, moved to Peachtree City where he joined a small law firm, met Jim and eventually joined him in the partnership.

The founding partners have never forgotten their love of small town America and have continued to be active in the local community. Jim has served as Chairman of the Fayette County Chamber of Commerce and held many other board and officer positions for several local civic organizations. Rick helped found the Fayette County Education Foundation, which raises money for local schools and teachers. He has served on numerous civic boards in Fayette and Fulton Counties.

Webb, Lindsey & Wade is located at 400 West Park Court, Suite 200 in Peachtree City, Georgia and at www.webb-firm.com.

Above: Attorneys and staff of Webb, Lindsey & Wade, LLC.

Below: Richard P. Lindsey.

BRENT SCARBROUGH & COMPANY, INC.

❖

Above: Coretta Scott King's Young Women's Leadership Academy site.

Below: Kia Plant, LaGrange.

Brent Scarbrough knew at an early age that he liked digging in the dirt and his love affair with the earth and the machines that move it has led him to a successful career as one of Georgia's premier site utility contractors, performing vital functions such as grading, clearing, erosion control, sewer, storm and water along with stream restoration and other related services for clients both large and small in the private and government sectors on the local, state and national levels.

Along the way he has garnered accolades and awards for his civic, community and environmental work. As an example in May 2008 he received a 2007 National Community Service Award from The National Utility Contractors Association NUCA) for

"…generous and creative community services projects planned and carried to fruition by contractor, associate and institutional members of NUCA…". The award was for four projects benefiting children and seniors for grading, landscaping and new equipment at Sam's School for special needs children, for children at Brooks United Methodist Church, for a safe gun range at Camp Thunder Boy Scout Camp and a new sewer line to the Fayette Senior Center for total donations of more than a quarter million dollars worth of work.

In the 1990s Brent's track record of providing quality service to wetland and stream mitigation projects won his company thirteen wetland jobs in thirteen years. These are now restored ecosystems that support a variety of wildlife, flood, storage and water quality measures. The projects total 1200 acres of restored, enhanced and presented wetlands and stream mitigation sites.

In 2002 the company began construction on the Flint River Mitigation Bank located in the upper Flint River watershed serving most of southside Atlanta.

Brent Scarbrough & Company began as a one man operation with a small silt fence business in Fayette County and has grown into a large operation doing business throughout the state and has now expanded into nine states. The firm now has more than 180 employees.

"Even though Brent is much larger now he still works very hard to keep a closeness with all his employees," his assistant, Laurie Vernon, emphasized.

The road to Brent Scarbrough's success began when he was a thirteen year old high school student in his native Fayette County, already driving tractors with the idea in mind he would one day enter the earth moving business. He learned how to operate heavy equipment on holidays and weekends working at Atlanta's Hartsfield Airport (now Hartsfield-Jackson Airport and the busiest airport in the nation).

It was in 1985, while in his junior year at Southern Polytechnic State University where he specialized in erosion control and silt fence installation that, with strong support from his family, Brent started a silt fence business which he sold several years later when his main focus became laying pipe.

When he decided to buy his first major piece of equipment for $40,000 it was considered a risky investment for a fledgling company by his sister, Dawn, and his friend and employee, Danny Huddleston. But it was the kind of decision they later agreed that put the company on the road to bigger success.

In 1988 the Scarbrough Company launched into underground utilities operations and has since become one of Georgia's larger underground utilities companies.

In 1994 the firm incorporated its Wetlands Mitigation Division, which now has the largest mitigation bank in the state in the Flint River drainage system. For over a decade Brent oversaw all aspects of the operation. In 1996, Shane Waters was brought in as vice president of operations to help guide the rapid growth of the company.

Over the past twenty-three years the company has experienced accelerated growth and in the past five years has doubled in size.

The Scarbrough Company is very much involved in the community, especially with youth programs which the company founder personally oversees.

Located at www.brentscarbrough.com and at 155 Robinson Drive in Fayetteville, Brent Scarbrough & Company remains one of Fayette County's most viable and visible home grown local corporations.

Above: Old mill at Crystal Lakes, in Fayetteville.

Below: Park Atlanta, parking lot for airport.

THE ROTARY CLUB OF PEACHTREE CITY

❖

*Above: Luther Glass, first club
president (right), accepting the Club
Charter from District Governor
Pratt Secrest.*

*Below: The past club presidents at the
Club's fortieth anniversary celebration
in November 2007. Back row (from
left to right): Ralph Jones, 1971-72;
Robert Neff, 1987-88; Dale Phenicie,
2002-03; David O'Rear, 2007-08;
and Charles Landrum, 2005-06.
Middle Row (from left to right):
Edwin Koons, 1978-79; John Vogel,
1979-80; John Kubitz, 1988-89;
Mary Chapman, 2006-07; Frances
Meaders, the Club's first female
president, 1993-94; Doc Jaleel, past
president of former South Fulton
Rotary Club; Jim Watkins, 1999-
2000; Gary McDermid, 1992-93;
Teresa Joiner, 1996-97; Costas
Soulakas, 2003-04; and Donna
Turner, 2001-02. Front Row (from left
to right): Bob Gasko, 1990-91; Eric
Maxwell, 2000-01; William "Bill"
MacDonald, 1995-96; and Mike
Smith, 1982-83.*

The Rotary Club of Peachtree City, currently one hundred and ten members strong, was chartered in November 1967, after local business and industrial leaders decided that Peachtree City needed a nationally chartered civic organization. The Club is the first organization of that kind in Fayette County.

The first honorary membership was presented to Joel Cowen in 1968, a former Georgia Tech student, who founded Peachtree City and served as its first mayor. In 2007 the Club turned forty where all past presidents were honored at a special event. Out of the original twenty-two members Ralph Jones is the only remaining charter member of the Club.

The Club has gained National and International recognition during the past four decades through its many community service projects. Its major project, the *Telephone Directory*, currently named the *Rotary Telephone Book*, has a distribution of over 50,000 copies to all homes and businesses in Fayette County at no charge.

First published in 1974 the phone book has allowed the club to make generous contributions to local, national and international projects through advertising proceeds. Since 1985 the World Community Service Projects made possible from the Phone Book proceeds coupled with matching funds from District and Rotary International, include: water wells, solar energy ovens, wheel chairs, books for the blind, computers, school supplies, and polio immunizations. Other projects supported by phone book proceeds include a contribution made to the Peachtree City Library for furnishings in a community room named for charter member and Past President Floy Farr.

The Club, sponsored by the Newnan Club, has sponsored the Fayetteville Club (1981) the Fayette Daybreak Club (1994) and the Fayette-Coweta Club (2007).

In 1987, Rotary International gave its authorization for the admission of women. Sponsored by charter member the late Floy Farr, Frances Meaders, long time Peachtree City Clerk, became the Club's first woman member and in 1993 became the Club's first woman president.

In 1994, at the annual district conference, the Club received the first of its many "Best Club" awards.

Great emphasis is placed on community service projects and programs involving children and young people, such as Literacy, Interact, GRSP, RYLA, Laws of Life and the Grand Prix Series.

Noteworthy projects and programs include:

- Organization and sponsorship of Interact Clubs, which function as youth rotary clubs, at McIntosh High School, Starr's Mill High School and the Counterpane School.
- Participation in the Georgia Rotary Student Program (GRSP) providing students from other countries the opportunity to study for one year at a Georgia college or university for the purpose of fostering goodwill and understanding through the youth.
- Annual sponsorship of rising high school juniors selected to receive the Rotary Youth Leadership Award based on their character and leadership abilities.
- Sponsorship of the Georgia Laws of Life Essay Contest, a character education program, in local middle and high schools.
- Sponsoring "Meet the Candidates" forums during elections to encourage greater voter participation.
- Monetary assistance for Alzheimer's research and participation in the annual Southern Crescent Alzheimer's Memory Walk.
- The Luther Glass Memorial Gazebo at Three Ponds on Peachtree Parkway.
- Establishing the Peachtree City Welcome Sign at Highways 54 and 74 for service organizations to display their logo.
- The Arnold Cheek Fishing Dock for Special Needs Children at Line Creek.
- Major contributor to the construction of the "Field of Hope", a little league facility for disabled or special needs children.
- The Howard Morgan Wetlands Nature Observatory near Crosstown Road.

- Sponsorship of the Souns program, a hands on literacy program for infants, toddlers and adults now widely supported by Rotary International.

In 2000, Past President Bill MacDonald was selected as the 2003-2004 term District Governor for District 6900. MacDonald is the first member from the Rotary Club of Peachtree City selected for this honor.

In 2005 the Club joined with the Peachtree City Running Club and began the Rotary Elementary School Grand Prix series to promote fitness through running for both youngsters and adults.

In 2007 the Dragon Boat Races and International Festival was held at Lake Peachtree. This successful fundraiser is now an annual event that supports local services while bringing the entire community together for a fun-filled day.

❖

Above: The 2008 Rotary Club members.

Below: A collection of the Rotary Club Telephone Book covers with several depicting projects completed in the community with funding from the telephone book.

TDK

TDK was founded in Tokyo, Japan, in 1935 to commercialize the magnetic material ferrite, which has allowed the company to develop a variety of valuable products to foster and advance the world's technological needs. Since then the company has expanded worldwide with manufacturing and distribution facilities throughout Asia, the Americas and Europe. Since 1979, TDK has chosen the fast growing Fayette County area to build a plant to distribute and produce recording media and ceramic capacitors, which are used in large quantities in mobile phones, flat-screen televisions and many other hi-tech products which serve society worldwide. There are a total of twelve TDK subsidiaries in the U.S. engaged in sales, research and development, and manufacturing. The plant located on TDK Boulevard in Peachtree City is one of the company's four manufacturing facilities located in the U.S.

TDK began in Peachtree City with the production of VCR cassette tapes. Chip capacitor production began in 1986 and continues today. Production of recordable compact disks began in 1995 and ended in 2001. In 2007, TDK's magnetic media business was spun-off to an allied company with production centering in Asia. TDK in Fayette County now has approximately 200 employees and is led by a team of Japanese and American managers.

Above: TDK Components USA, Inc., was awarded the US-EPA 2008 Performance Track Environmental Performance Award. This award reflects the commitment of TDK employees to continuous improvement in environmental performance and stewardship.

Below: Since 2002, TDK Components has observed Patriot Day with the flying of the American Flag.

In today's digital and information age, TDK fully utilizes its core technologies to develop a wide range of products, from hard disk drive heads, multilayer ceramic chip capacitors, inductors and sensors, to noise management parts and others. These products have been essential in the manufacture of mobile equipment and information appliances.

When TDK was established, the company was named Tokyo Denki Kagaku Kogyo Co., Ltd. This name came from the fact that Dr. Yogoro Kato and Dr. Takeshi Takei, the inventors of ferrite, worked at the Electric (Denki) Chemistry (Kagaku) Faculty of the Tokyo Institute of Technology. The company name, TDK, was derived from the Department of Electrochemistry (Denki Kagaku) at Tokyo Institute of Technology.

TDK's corporate mark is a geometric design representing the point to point connections in the electronic industry between computers and magnetic materials and symbolizes the entire TDK group's commitment to the quality of the firm's products and services.

From the initial production of ferrite cores, TDK has developed a broad range of products and has experienced tremendous growth, a growth based on the company's founding spirit and expressed in the corporate

motto, "Contribute to the culture and industry through creativity."

The company's strength lies in the abundant materials technologies it has developed over the years and the substantial process expertise that utilize the technology effectively.

The commercialization of ceramic materials in the manufacture of capacitors in the early 1950s is an example of TDK leveraging its expertise in basic materials to maintain its leadership in the electronics business. Due to the high demand for wireless communication in the 1940s the ferrite core business boomed, and in the early 1950s the shortage of ceramic capacitors presented an opportunity for the company to produce ceramic capacitors. The demand for radios also increased rapidly, resulting in the demand for transformers that included ferrite products and ceramic capacitors.

The electronics industry is the core of TDK's business. The company is in a constant state of transition to adapt to the major changes in this fast changing industry. TDK sees the rapid spread of computers and data networking as a new era of opportunity.

TDK's intermediate business plans call for strengthening manufacturing capability and growing customers through developing custom products, operational excellence, optimum allocation and use of resources.

The company's corporate citizenship activities concentrate on academics, research and education, sports, art and culture, environmental conservation, social welfare and local community activities.

Above: TDK Components USA, Inc., plant in Peachtree City.

Below: Multilayer ceramic chip capacitors produced by TDK Components USA have contributed greatly to the miniaturization of electronic devices. Video cameras use about 300 chip capacitors, while cellular phones use about 200.

ATLANTIC TAPE & DISTRIBUTING

When Richard Lawrimore's job was "downsized" in 1975, he decided it was time to go into business for himself, even though the economy was shaky at the time. "When you start during a recession, there's no place to go but up," he believes.

Because of his experience in the tape business, Lawrimore took out a mortgage on his home, bought some used machinery, and started his own line of retail packaging. "The machinery we were able to buy was so antiquated and slow that a friend watching us roll tape asked why we thought we were going to run 3M out of business," he recalls.

Atlantic Tape & Distributing started business in small, rented quarters, but, in 1980, the company was able to purchase a 4,000 square foot building at 1128 Highway 54 in Fayetteville. After only a year in the new building, it was necessary to purchase an adjoining 2,000 square foot building. That building has now been expanded five times, providing a total of 38,000 square feet.

As business continued to grow, Atlantic Tape, with a group of businessmen, purchased a 290,000 square foot building located on Highway 74 South in Peachtree City in 2008, known now as Atlantic Center. Atlanta Tape Company will utilize 80,000 plus square feet, sharing the building with other businesses and with space to lease out. "Our need after thirty-three years was twofold," explains Lawrimore. "One, get into a highly developed industrial area that was growing, such as Peachtree City; and, two, to have a building that would give us the

space for growth and the credibility of being in business for thirty-three years."

Peachtree City is one of the fastest growing cities in Georgia and has been successful in acquiring major manufacturers to the already large industrial area that, fortunately, has room for more new growth.

Atlantic Tape & Distributing was founded to serve the retail market through packaged pressure sensitive tapes. "When you start on a shoestring, you build one new employee at a time, one new machine at a time," comments Lawrimore.

Lawrimore soon realized the company's potential to become a major supplier of industrial tapes and other products. Since that

Above: We maintain various sizes of foam, bubble wrap and peanuts. Bubble and foam are available in various widths, lengths and perforated by special order.

Below: Atlantic Center is a 290,000 square foot building. A group of businessmen purchased this facility, remodeled it and Atlantic Tape Company occupies close to 80,000 square feet with room to grow.

time, the company has intensified its efforts with a commitment to professional service and quality products that ensure the best cost savings for its customers.

"Price is always a factor, but there must be service and the ability to stay abreast of a changing market with the desire to meet the challenge with ideas that will benefit the customer," says Lawrimore.

The company's focus over the years has been to expand its product base in order to better serve the industrial trade. Atlantic Tape has added various machines for packaging, carton sealing, and stretch wrapping systems, along with both plastic and steel strapping machines. To compliment the tape and packaging products, Atlantic Tape has added a complete line of janitorial, maintenance and sanitary supplies.

Atlantic Tape's distribution and sales office in Peachtree City is dedicated to providing a quick response to any technical expertise needed. The company has taken a leadership position by specializing in products for industrial use and has an understanding of the customer's need to improve their bottom line.

The company now employs twenty-four people, including sales representatives in Arkansas and Athens, Georgia. The customer base has grown to more than 3,000 and annual sales now total $11 million. An expansion that will add a complete box line to the existing product mix is expected to add significantly to the sales growth.

Lawrimore and the Atlantic Tape employees are involved in a number of charitable organizations, including St. Jude Hospital, Smile Train, the Salvation Army, St. Joseph Indian School and others.

For additional information about Atlantic Tape & Distributing, visit the website at www.atlantictape.com.

Above: We handle numerous brands of stretch file; this area is mainly Intertape product in hand and machine widths.

Below: This area is Signma stretch film both in machine and hand film.

BRAY PROPERTIES, LLLP

Huie L. Bray, born and reared in Fayette County, is one of its pioneer developers and business and civic leaders.

Upon his returned from World War II in the mid 1940s, he began as a construction worker with an uncle in downtown Atlanta where he fondly remembers working on such classic landmark buildings as the old Peachtree Arcade and Biltmore Hotel. "That was the beginning of my construction and building career," he recalls.

It was a career that has spanned more than six decades and has seen unprecedented growth and progress in Fayette County and the metro area. "Mr. Huie" as he came to be known by his many friends and business associates over the years, has been an integral part of that progress, building many of the first developments in the county.

Beginning with a masonry business in 1947 when his total assets were "a 1940 Chevrolet, one homemade trailer, some hand tools and $250 in cash," he built one of Fayette County's most successful enterprises, diversifying into building homes, commercial buildings, service stations, church additions and self-storage facilities, which today are the mainstay of Bray Properties, LLLP, along with Bray's Corner and some commercial properties.

Today the company has more than 176 thousand square feet of rental space consisting of over 800 storage units and offices with five full time employees.

It was in 1978 when he built Fayette Self Storage, the first of its kind to serve the south side of Atlanta. The facility, which is still owned and operated by Bray Properties, has approximately 800 units, including spaces for boat and recreational vehicle parking. Over the years the company has built and sold several self-storage facilities in other parts of the metro area.

The Bray name is synonymous with home building in Fayette County. "In 1952-53, I built the first new home in the county for Ray and Joan Neal," he relates. "Joan still lives in the house on Forest Avenue." His company went on to build homes throughout the area, including the first two new homes in the new Peachtree City in 1959.

With growth in Fayette County beginning to accelerate in the 1950s "Mr. Huie" obtained his state real estate license and concentrated his efforts on the local real estate market.

The company's first subdivision was Blakely Woods, Fayetteville's first new development following World War II. Bray also built the Stonewall Apartments, another first in Fayetteville and the county.

In the early days when there was little construction going on in Fayette County, because he was recognized as one of the area's better builders, he was approached about building service stations in Atlanta. The company built many of the city's independent service stations and also built them throughout the area for major oil companies.

As a Fayette native Huie Bray has seen being involved in civic, community and church affairs as an important part of his life and a way to give back to his home county.

Working with the local Boy Scouts has been one of his long-time and most rewarding projects.

He has served on the all important local planning and zoning commission, helping to draft the county's first building and zoning codes. He was the first zoning administrator. Also, he served as both the volunteer Fire Chief and EMS Director. From their inception in 1953 he has been an active member of local Kiwanis Clubs.

An important business involvement has been his many years of volunteering with the Home Builders Association of Metro Atlanta where he also was chairman of the Home Building Show in Atlanta.

He has been married to the former Bea Teate since 1953 and they have two children, Danny "Bo" and Patsy, and many grandchildren and great grandchildren.

Since 1960, he has been a faithful member of the Fayetteville First Baptist Church and has served on both the long range planning and building committees.

"God has been good to me and my family, allowing us to be successful and in turn allowing me to serve Fayette County," he concludes.

GLOBAL AERO LOGISTICS INC.

Peachtree City's Global Aero Logistics, Inc., which until 2005 was named World Airways, now a wholly owned subsidiary of the company, is a leading international cargo and passenger charter business built on a rich heritage of aviation tradition and innovation that began in 1948.

World Airways moved to 101 World Drive in 2001; this later became the holding company headquarters as well. Global's other subsidiary, North American Airlines, operates charter passenger service from its base at JFK International Airport in New York.

The company has provided charter airline service continuously for sixty years. In 1950 entrepreneur Edward J. Daly bought the fledgling airline for $50,000. It began a long and storied history of serving the U.S. military, beginning with airlifts during the Korean conflict in the early 1950s and assisting world humanitarian causes when the company helped refugees escape during the Hungarian revolution in 1956. Following the end of the

airlift, World received a contract from the military to provide daily inter-island service in support of U.S. troops in the western Pacific. World played a major role during the Vietnam War by moving military personnel and materials across the Pacific.

By the late 1960s, World had a fleet of six newly acquired Boeing 727-100s, five 707-373Cs and had broken ground on the World Air Center at Oakland International Airport in Oakland, California. In 1971 the company bought three Douglas DC-8-63CF convertible freighters and added three more in 1973 along with a Boeing 747-272C nose-loading convertible aircraft.

In March 1975, Daly took two 727s to Saigon to make twenty evacuation flights from Da Nang under government charter. When the U.S. Embassy canceled the contract, Daly directed two 727s to Da Nang to rescue women and children, although only one flight landed. The "Last Flight From Da Nang" garnered worldwide media attention as Daly and the World crew fought off a horde of would-be passengers seeking refuge on the aircraft, dodged bullets and grenades and ultimately carried more than 300 people to safety in Saigon.

Shortly after that event, Daly ordered the evacuation of fifty-seven orphans from Saigon onboard a World DC-8, triggering the launch of Operation Babylift, which ultimately rescued approximately 3,000 Vietnamese orphans before the fall of Saigon.

Following deregulation of the airline industry in 1978, World became one of the first scheduled low-fare airlines, operating for six years from its headquarters and hub in Oakland, before returning to charter-only service. The company subsequently added the first Boeing 747 freighter and ordered six McDonnell Douglas DC-10-30 aircraft.

As World returned to its charter roots in the late 1980s, it operated a single aircraft type, the DC-10-30, and concentrated on serving the military as well as tour operators and other airlines. This strategy proved successful and World expanded its fleet again in the early 1990s with the addition of new McDonnell Douglas MD-11 aircraft. The MD-11s, in both passenger and cargo configuration, allowed World to offer even greater capability to its customers.

World has been a leading provider of passenger and cargo support for the U.S. military for more than fifty years, not only during peacetime, but also during conflicts such as the war on terrorism in Afghanistan and Operation Iraqi Freedom. The airline also is known for providing humanitarian flights at critical times to such places as Bosnia and Somalia.

Today's fleet of twenty wide-body MD-11, DC-10 and Boeing 747 aircraft operate around the world, serving the Air Mobility Command for the U.S. military and providing contract air service for commercial passenger and cargo customers on five continents.

The company has approximately 2500 employees, with a revenue base of more than $1 billion. Customer base is primarily U.S. military troop transport, cargo operations for international airlines, and a variety of airline or tour operators that require large passenger aircraft.

A strong supporter of local and state community affairs, the company supports the American Cancer Society, Alzheimer's Association, Fayette Community Foundation, Partners in Education (Fayette County Education Foundation), the American Red Cross, USO of Georgia, Great Georgia Airshow and Boy Scouts of America (Flint River Council).

BF Inkjet Media, Inc., a local family owned business, is a leader and award winner in its field of manufacturing core products, which are the result of the firm's expertise and innovation in creating artist canvas and other high-end art products used in Wide Format ink jet printing.

Wade says, "We live by the motto, 'Where Excellence is a Habit, Perfection is a Goal'."

Due to Wade's expertise and unparalleled ability to go from laboratory to production, BF Inkjet is able to meet the needs of all of its customers. "We believe that our success has been based on giving each person or

The company was founded in 1992 by Max Bowers. It developed the inkjet coating process for inkjet receptive canvas and vinyl, which was later patented.

Originally the firm was involved in the development of photographic coatings at another location. Wade Bowers is the principal chemist and developer of all formulations as well as the R & D and Production Director. Commenting on the firm's emphasis on quality

organization we deal with value and respect for the time and money they have invested," Wade commented. "We are committed to consistently producing the highest quality products available backed by impeccable customer service and personal attention."

Construction on the coating machine, which is the heart of the company's business, began in 1996 and full production started in 1998. The firm's growth and expansion has

continued at a steady pace and today is a leader in the field.

Indicative of the high regard the company is held in the digital imaging industry, BF Inkjet was awarded the Digital Imaging Marketing Associates (DIMA) Innovative Product Award for Black and White Photo Canvas in 2008.

The firm also produces a wide product offering in banner, sign, poster and presentation materials compatible with most current ink and printer systems, both for indoor and outdoor applications.

"We are committed to constantly improving our products and services because we recognize we cannot grow and accomplish our company objectives without satisfying our customers." Max emphasized. "It is our daily practice and goal to treat each of our customers, employees and suppliers with the highest level of flexibility, dignity and trust for the role each plays in our progress as an organization."

Located at 116 Bethea Road in Fayetteville, BF Inkjet prides itself in being a family run company. BF stands for Bowers Family.

CITY OF PEACHTREE AND PEACHTREE CITY TOURISM ASSOCIATION

❖

Above: Civic sign welcomes residents and visitors alike. Peachtree City has a long history of civic involvement and volunteer spirit.

Middle: Peachtree City's annual Memorial Day Celebration features a parade of golf carts paying tribute to those lost in service to our country.

Bottom right: The fountain located at City Hall Plaza was donated by a group of Japanese industries located in and around Peachtree City.

Peachtree City's history is an unusual and fascinating story. It was in the late 1950s when an Augusta builder, Pete Knox, and a Fayette County banker, Floy Farr, chose a precocious Georgia Tech student, Joel Cowan, to plan and build a new kind of town near Fayette County's Shakerag Community.

The back story is like something out of a movie. Knox's son was a Tech student and Cowan was his roommate. The developer and banker were so impressed with Cowan they entrusted him with what would become a multi-million dollar project, the building of Peachtree City. When it was realized by Knox and his partners the project was going to require more capital than they had planned, Cowan found the necessary funds from Phipps Land Company. He later became the city's first mayor.

"Joel brought in planners, as well as being a good planner himself," said Farr "and he made the new preplanned city work. He oversaw the project with a steady hand, always sticking to the original plan of only allowing a certain

percentage of land a year to be developed. If you look at the original plan of Peachtree City you can clearly see that what was written down then is there today."

Although modified over the years to reduce Peachtree City's eventual size from 80,000 residents to the current projection of 40,000 residents, the city has developed according to Cowan's original plan for the past fifty years and at 36,000 residents is ninety percent complete. It has retained its unique village concept, with a commercial center surrounded by varying styles and price ranges of housing, interspersed with recreational amenities and schools.

In 1979, Equitable Life Assurance Society of the United States (lender to Phipps) went through a friendly foreclosure and took possession of the undeveloped property, hiring Douglas B. Mitchell's Peachtree City

Development Corporation to continue developing the project. The major growth occurred in the 1980s and 1990s when Jerry Peterson was the planner for PCDC. Mitchell and his then-partner, Steve Black, bought the remaining undeveloped land from Equitable in about 1994. During most of this time, Jim Williams served as the city planner for the city of Peachtree City.

There are currently five villages in the city, and the names reflect some of the history of Fayette County. Aberdeen Village developed primarily in the 1960s, and was named for the old Aberdeen community in the area. Glenloch Village developed primarily in the 1970s, and was named to acknowledge the adjacent lake. Braelinn Village, developed in the 1980s, continues the Scottish theme, and Kedron Village, developed primarily in the 1990s, reflects another community in the County's history (Kidron). The fifth and final village, Wilksmoor, is under development now and was named to acknowledge the Wilks family and Wilks Grove Baptist Church located in that area, with the Scottish "moor" suffix.

Although Peachtree City is now known nationwide for its hallmark golf cart paths, they were not part of the original plan. Today the city has a ninety mile network of paved multi-use paths that serve as the city's alternate transportation system, carrying pedestrians, bicyclists and golf carters from residential neighborhoods to area schools, shopping centers and recreational events and activities.

The paths were first installed by the developer to connect residents in the Golf View neighborhood to the nearby Flat Creek Golf Course. Additional neighborhoods were linked in to the system as they were developed. The city later adopted requirements that all new development link to the system or provide access for future connections. Along the way, the city had to request legislation from the state of Georgia authorizing local communities to allow and regulate the use of golf carts on public streets (1974).

Among the city's many amenities are 3 private golf courses, 2 lakes, a 2500 seat open air amphitheater, a state-of-the-art tennis center, 5 public pools, over 50 athletic fields, a public BMX track, a skate park, a dog park and 17 playgrounds and tot lots.

Above: From the 1957 prospectus for Peachtree City, a conceptual idea of what Lake Peachtree might have looked like.

Middle: From the 1957 Business Prospectus for Peachtree City, a conceptual idea of Peachtree City's industrial park, including an airport (which is there) and a cloverleaf at the intersection of State Highways 54 and 74 (which, alas, is not).

Bottom: Overlooking Flat Creek Golf Course in Aberdeen Village.

RINNAI AMERICA

Above: Rinnai Peachtree City Headquarters.

Below: Rinnai research lab in Peachtree City.

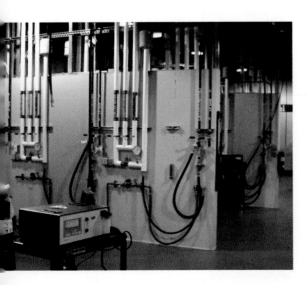

Rinnai, the world's largest manufacturer of gas appliances, moved its North American operations from nearby LaGrange to Peachtree City in 2001 to facilitate its international and domestic travel requirements by being closer to the nation's largest airport, Hartsfield-Jackson International.

The Peachtree City operation is comprised of distribution, training and research facilities for the United States, Canada and Mexico. Other U.S. offices are in California, Florida and Texas.

The Rinnai Corporation founded in Nagoya, Japan, in 1920 by the Naito and Hayashi families is world renowned for its award-winning, industry-leading, continuous flow tankless water heater.

Rinnai's North American operations are mainly responsible for marketing the application solutions and distribution of the company's innovative products and enjoy relationships with a wide range of leading sales partners across the continent. Those leading the Peachtree City operation are President Yuzo Yoshida and General Manager Phillip Weeks along with talented and dedicated employees and a dynamic management team.

Since its inception in 1975, Rinnai's North American operations have grown from distributing spa heaters to marketing and distribution of an extensive product line that today includes portable cook tops, commercial grade rice cookers, smokeless griddles, vent-free and direct-vent gas heaters and a tankless water heating system, available for both residential and commercial installations. Over the last five years, Rinnai North America has consistently produced double digit growth in the U.S., a milestone it attributes to total customer commitment and delivering an unparalleled Whole House Solution for heating water and air.

Rinnai's signature product, the tankless water heater, has models for applications with single units supplying up to 9.8 gallons of hot water per minute continuously for as long as hot water is needed. The heaters are up to thirty percent more energy efficient than a traditional natural gas tank water heater and up to fifty percent more efficient than an electric tank water heater.

Today, Rinnai is the technology leader in its industry. Annual corporate revenues, including those of its subsidiaries, are in excess of $2 billion USD. With a global perspective to create twenty-first century products for the home and business, Rinnai Corporation has committed itself to producing lifestyle-enhancing products that incorporate the latest technological innovations with energy and environmental concerns.

The Peachtree City location is at 103 International Drive. For additional information regarding the products, service or locations near you, visit www.rinnai.us.

All-Lift of Georgia, Inc., was founded in 1988 to provide the Atlanta area with a reliable and experienced business partner for all their equipment needs. All-Lift offers new Clark forklifts as well as a large selection of late model reconditioned lifts, rentals, used attachments and a full line of material handling equipment.

All-Lift was organized after Barry Naulls moved from Tampa, Florida, to manage a Jonesboro-based forklift company, only to discover the company was in serious financial trouble. Although he had very little capital, Naulls purchased a used van and started a forklift service company in Riverdale, Georgia. The company grew and moved to Fayetteville in 1991.

Naulls, the president and sole shareholder of All-Lift, has more than forty years experience in the forklift industry. He began in 1966 as a mechanic and has held key management positions with large corporations within the industry, including top sales rep in North America and president of Hansler Industries.

Jimmy Schwab of Fayetteville joined the company in its early years and has been a key part of the firm's growth. He has held many positions within the company, including operations manager.

All-Lift received a boost in business after Naulls realized the air freight business at the airport was a twenty-four hour, seven days a week operation and began offering the same hours. All-Lift quickly became known as the company to call after 5:00 p.m.

All-Lift became the Clark Forklift distributor for central and south Georgia in 2003. John Carruthers, considered the top Clark parts manager in the country, joined All-Lift at that time. Jerry Travis, a Fayette native and top Clark sales rep with more than thirty years experience, joined All-Lift in 2005 and has helped put the company on the map.

All-Lift is located in the Kenwood Business Park off Georgia highway 85. The company owns two buildings and has more than 25,000 square feet of office and warehouse space. A branch facility is located in Macon, Georgia.

All-Lift has a base of more than a thousand customers and has enjoyed continuous, controlled growth since its founding.

All-Lift of Georgia is located at 175 Carnes Drive in Fayetteville and on the Internet at www.alllifeofgeorgia.com.

LAW OFFICES OF LEE MASON

Fayetteville attorney Lee Mason specializes only in real estate and community association law. Developers, homeowners associations and individuals turn to Mason for his expertise in this specialty niche of the law.

Mason also offers complete management services to homeowners and condominium associations. His management company, Community Association Management, LLC (CAM), is ranked year after year in the *Atlanta Business Chronicle Book of Lists* as one of Georgia's top community association management companies.

Through CAM, Mason is able to greatly simplify the operations of neighborhood associations by combining legal and managerial services into one setting. Usually, associations must hire a management company for day to day operations, and an attorney for any legal issues that might arise. Mason's clients get complete managerial services along with the advice and counsel of an experienced real estate and community association attorney.

"Combining management and legal services is a unique concept," Mason said. "With us, you receive both services for one set fee. It's what sets us apart in this industry."

CAM handles all of the finances for associations, including paying vendors, collecting association dues and reconciling the association's bank accounts each month. The company also drives through neighborhoods to check for covenant violations. Going to court to enforce covenant restrictions and collecting outstanding homeowner association dues is a routine practice for Mason.

"Having a strong homeowners association with quality management and legal services protects investments for all homeowners," Mason said. "It ensures that property values increase rather than decrease over time."

Asked why he became an attorney he said, "I have always been interested in all areas of law, including the three branches of government. I worked with a real estate law firm prior to applying for law school and was convinced this was the career I wanted to pursue." His alternative occupation is accounting. Hobbies include swimming, playing tennis with his family, working out and playing hand bells at church.

Mason's affiliations are with the State Bar of Georgia, American Bar Association, Fayette County Bar Association, licensed Georgia real estate broker, national and Georgia Chapter of the Community Associations Institute, Professional Community Association, Manager (PCAM) Association Management Specialist and Certified Manager of Community Associations.

The offices of Community Association Management are located at 101 Devant Street, Suites 904 and 905 in Fayetteville. Additional information is available at www.camga.com.

On March 8, 1940, Delta Employees Credit Union was founded by eight employees of Delta Air Lines to serve as an additional benefit to employees. Through the years the credit union expanded its field of membership to include the extended family of members, subsidiaries of Delta Air Lines, and employees of select companies and residents of counties in the metro-Atlanta area.

In October 2005 the credit union became Delta Community Credit Union, signifying not only its ongoing connection with Delta Air Lines but also its new focus on the community. Today the credit union has more than 175,000 members and is the largest credit union in Georgia. Delta Community is a state-chartered credit union, organized under the Georgia Department of Banking and Finance and federally-insured by the National Credit Union Administration.

Due to its large concentration of members in the area, the credit union opened its first community branch in Fayette County in July of 2003 in the Peachtree City Braelinn Village Shopping Center. In January of 2006, a second branch in Fayetteville at Summit Point was opened, and in March of 2007, a third branch in Peachtree City at Wisdom Road was opened. The President and CEO, Rick Foley, has been a resident of Fayette County since 1974.

Delta Community's corporate mission is to be responsive to the financial needs of members by providing high quality services in an environment of trust, care, and financial strength. Profits are returned to members in the form of attractive interest rates and dividends. The credit union works hard to continually bring members the best financial products and services available anywhere, including no-fee checking, investment services and extensive online banking services.

Delta Community Credit Union is a strong, safe and smart place to entrust your money. Not only is it a great place to save and a friendly place to bank, it offers innovative and industry-leading financial products that make it the perfect place to conduct financial business. Delta Community is excited to be a part of this thriving county and plans to continue to branch out in Fayette.

Additional information on Delta Community Credit Union is available by visiting www.deltacommunitycu.com.

❖

Above: Peachtree City-Wisdom Road Branch.

Below: President and CEO Rick Foley.

PASCAL'S BISTRO

In its short but storied history Pascal's Bistro has become one of Peachtree City's most popular places where the diverse and local clientele from Fayette and surrounding counties come to enjoy classical continental cuisine and celebrate special events.

When Karen and Pascal LeCorre opened the Bistro in 1999 it was the fulfillment of a long-time goal to have their own restaurant. They were the perfect combination, she with a business background and Pascal, a chef.

Featuring dishes which offer classic takes on fish, beef, pork, lamb and poultry, it was only a short time before Pascal's was doing a brisk business.

Located in Peachtree City's popular Westpark Walk Shopping Center, the restaurant is easily accessible to Fayette Countians and clientele in the surrounding area. "Our clientele is very loyal," Karen commented. "A number of couples have gotten engaged at our restaurant and then celebrated their anniversaries in subsequent years."

The Bistro's eclectic menu and attentive service draw rave reviews from customers: "This was one of the best dining experiences I've had," one customer exclaimed. "The food was amazing, very friendly atmosphere and the service was superb," another commented. "Love their lunch; it's fresh and varied. Dinner also is delicious." Pascal's popular pasta Lunch Buffet features four types of pasta and fourteen different meats and fresh vegetables. For a list of the wonderful appetizers, entrees, and wines, visit www.pascalsbistro.com.

Waxing eloquent about his classic Steak Au Poivre, Chef LeCorre said, "It is probably a century old and, like Mozart's music, it is perfect. It is delish." The rice in his signature baked Flounder comes from Thailand and the fish is stuffed with a crab cake. "Who would have thought that Thai rice, Spanish saffron and American crab cakes could possibly be so good together," he enthused.

Over the past decade the LeCorres and their staff have become an integral part of the Fayette County scene and support many community and charitable projects.

"We plan to serve the community for many years to come," the couple pledged.

TNT-TECHNOLOGIES, INC.

It began in 1986 with local friends and family helping each other with their technology needs. Today, TNT-Technologies, Inc., which moved its operations in 1997 to Peachtree City from Fort Lauderdale, Florida, provides a variety of Information Technologies to clients throughout North America, the Caribbean and Europe.

Speaking of the early days and how the company has grown, founder Tony DellaTorre commented, "Client references have been the cornerstone of our business. As we continued to grow in size and with new technology, we went from working on the bits and bytes of hardware to the analytics of Financial Business Intelligence processes."

Two key people who are instrumental to TNT are Tony's wife, Rachel, and Luiz Oliveira.

"During the past twenty-three years we had to evolve to keep up with technology," Della Torre elaborates. "We started as an infrastructure business working with server hardware and networks. We evolved to data structure and data warehousing. Natural progression has taken us to Business Intelligence and finally to our current focus of Financial Analytics and Reporting."

In the mid 1990s the company experienced a growth surge in our infrastructure business. The early 2000s saw TNT have another surge in growth as it played a more critical role in the Business Intelligence market place.

"Today, our clients range from the financial services industry to the manufacturing space and everything in between," DellaTorre points out.

Within the financial analytical market, Corporate Performance Management (CPM) has matured and with the recent acquisition of the CPM market by the ERP market, our plan for the future is to lead in the evolution and corporate driven strategic implementations of CPM. "We have leveraged the experience gained from implementing hundreds of applications to provide unparallel services and solutions," he adds.

True to its roots as a family values company, TNT supports local civic and community projects, including local schools and children's sports teams.

For more information on TNT-Technologies, you may visit www.tnt-technologies.com.

THE LEE CENTER

The Lee Center, founded and developed in the mid-1970s, by the father and son team, Julian H. Lee, Sr., and Julian H. Lee, Jr., was Fayette's first industrial and retail development primarily designed to provide affordable, well-maintained warehouse and retail space for lease to local small to medium size businesses. Today the Center has grown from a single warehouse built in 1975 to fifteen mixed-use buildings encompassing more than three hundred thousand square feet serving both industrial and retail business.

The development began when Julian, Sr., purchased the property on which it now sits, in a mostly rural Fayette County, for use as a pasture to raise his many horses. Being a man of vision with an entrepreneurial spirit, Julian, Sr., could see that the Fayetteville area was on the cusp of industrial and commercial growth and in 1970 had the property rezoned. He then partnered with his son to build the first building on the property, which was completed in 1975.

Julian, Sr., continued to work diligently at his denture practice in Atlanta, while his son and daughter-in-law Donna committed to the process of developing and managing the complex. Julian, Jr., with his experience in building and architecture and his wife, Donna, with her expertise in business management and accounting, continued to plan and develop the complex by adding approximately one building every two to three years. In order to provide an appealing entrance into the Lee Center and into the city of Fayetteville, the Lee's overall plan included the design of three brick storefronts that face Highway 314. The family successfully completed the development with a total of fifteen buildings by October 2002.

In April 2005, due to the tragic untimely loss of Julian, Jr., in a boating accident, Donna took over as general managing partner. Today, the Lee Center continues to be a family business with the Lee children, Julie Orndorff, Jeremiah Lee, and Jillian Lee serving as limited partners while working along side their mom, Donna, to continue the family tradition.

The Lee Center is located on Georgia Highway 314 and Bethea Road in Fayetteville and at www.theleecenter.com.

The Southern Federal Credit Union was established in 1963 when a small group of Federal Aviation Administration (FAA) employees on Atlanta's south side decided to form a credit union to pool their savings and make loans to one another. Over the past five decades the Southern Federal Credit Union has continued to grow, and today the organization serves over 250 employer groups and offers a wide variety of financial products and services.

The credit union began operations with one employee and eleven members, and today serves approximately 29,000 members with a staff of more than eighty employees in Fayette County. Southern serves members nationwide, with employer groups located mainly on Atlanta's south side. The majority of members and employer groups are located in Fayette, Coweta, Clayton and Spalding Counties, and since 1992 the organization's headquarters have been located at 430 East Lanier Avenue in Fayetteville.

As a full-service financial institution the Southern offers a complete range of financial products and services to its members: regular savings accounts; checking accounts; ATM and Visa check cards; money market accounts; traditional and Roth IRAs; certificates of deposit; Christmas and vacation club accounts; Visa credit cards (classic, gold and platinum); loans on new and used autos; recreational vehicle loans; all types of mortgage loans and lines of credit; website access for online banking and bill pay; electronic statements; safe deposit boxes; twenty-four hour automated telephone account access and even a personal car-buying service.

THE SOUTHERN FEDERAL CREDIT UNION

The Southern began a major expansion in 1985 when it extended membership to Chick-fil-A's corporate office employees, U.S. Customs employees, Atlantic Southeast Airlines, contractors within the FAA and Southern Mills employees and their immediate family members. In 1987 the Southern completed its first merger with the Sherwin Williams Credit Union and in the following years merged with the credit unions of Atlanta Federal Penitentiary, Griffin Spalding and Tara.

As of second quarter 2008 the Southern is managing assets in excess of $211 million and operating branches in Fayetteville, Peachtree City, Griffin, Jonesboro and Newnan.

Looking to the future, Southern officials pledged to continue to "look for new and better ways of providing financial services for our members."

❖

Above: Main office of The Southern Federal Credit Union in Fayetteville.

Below: The Peachtree City branch of The Southern Federal Credit Union.

PAUL C. ODDO, SR.

When the late Paul C. Oddo, Sr. (1915-2008), and his wife, Genevieve, decided to escape cold Minnesota winters in 1970 by moving their small book publishing business and family to southern climes, they chose what was then the bucolic Fayette County Seat, Fayetteville, which quickly became one of metro Atlanta's prime business and commercial destinations.

Oddo Publishing, Inc., a publisher of children's supplementary educational readers, thrived in its new environment. With help from wife Genevieve as editor, and sons, Paul, Jr., Charles and Warren, the company's books were award winners. Freedoms Foundation presented an award in 1978 and 1988 for best children's book on Americana. The McGuffey Award followed in 1999.

The business operated from the now famous Robert K. Price "Quonset" huts and sold books throughout the United States, Canada and Japan.

With the backing of their father, the sons also became successful Fayette County businessmen. They branched into public accounting, a restaurant and even raised cattle.

Paul, Sr., believed in the community and invested his time, energy and money into it. He was instrumental in aiding the progress of his adopted city and county by bringing much needed quality commercial development to the south side of Fayetteville.

Active throughout his ninety-three years, he did not retire from business until he was eighty-nine. During his long and productive life he was active in civic and religious affairs in the community.

Paul, Jr., founded Paul C. Oddo, Jr., P.C., in 1979 after having worked for major Atlanta CPA firms such as Price Waterhouse. The firm began doing business as Oddo Brothers CPAs in the early 1990s.

In 1996 the Oddo family entered the restaurant business, building the popular GTOs Fabulous 50s Drive-in on family property on Highway 85. Today the successor to that restaurant is a Starbucks.

By the end of the twentieth century the Oddo family business legacy could be seen on former family land where kudzu and hay once grew. This pastoral scene has been replaced by a Kroger shopping center and national retailers like Walgreens, Chick-fil-A, McDonalds and a Wachovia Bank.

Commenting on his family's dedication to the community Paul, Jr., said, "We always intended to be good neighbors who provided quality products, services and development. To the extent we achieved that goal, it was through hard work and Divine Assistance."

Below: The Oddo family in front of their house: Charles, Genevieve, Paul, Jr., Paul, Sr., and Warren. c. 1982.

❖

*Above: Peachtree Editorial Service
Staff: Row I; Sarah Shaffer, Kelly
Landsiedel, and Judy Walker. Row 2:
Carolyn Trousdale, Cindy Van Wert,
Tammy Vena, Betty Miller, JoAnne
Holt, and Rhonda Jones. Row 3: Vicki
Oakley, Kristin Haggerty, Terri
Hartman, Kathy Martin, and Cindy
Peach. Not pictured: Susan
Fitzgerald, Lynn Horton, Patti
Adams, and Meagan Mason.*

*Below: Doug and June Gunden,
founders of Peachtree Editorial
Service, one of Fayette County's and
the country's most unique businesses.*

Although the word unique is often overused and misused, it certainly applies to Peachtree Editorial & Proofreading Service, the nation's only company known to specialize in proofreading English Bibles before going to press.

Doug and June Gunden, both of whom had previously worked for Christian publishing firms, began the company in the early 1980s in their home. The company has grown to a staff of twenty, working from a Peachtree City office.

Commenting on why such a unique service is needed, June said, "The English Bible exists in many translations and each is contained on a database. When that database is used to create a printed page, a typesetter uses software to interpret the data and flow it onto templates. Because neither the typesetter nor the software is infallible, proofreaders are needed to ensure that all the text is there and is formatted correctly."

Doug explains why the company's work is so specialized: "First of all, because of the uniqueness of the Bible itself, our work is different from that of a proofreader or editor of other material. Each word and each mark of punctuation has been meticulously studied by scholars and may not be altered in the printing process. Second, because there are so many different versions, it takes an intentional effort to learn the specialized information about each one and to be sure that, with the different design of each Bible, the Scripture text is still intact."

Doug goes on to say that since the Bible is the best selling book in the world, many publishers want to have a part in it. They often offer not only the translation itself, but additions such as study notes, devotional material, cross references, artwork, and other supplements. All of these help readers to engage the Scripture text and as a result more lives are touched by its power.

The company reads more than seventy-five Bibles each year for companies all over the United States and England.

FAYETTE COUNTY BOARD OF EDUCATION

From its beginnings in the late 1800s, the Fayette County School System established a nurturing environment with the goal of providing its students with the highest quality education. The school system, with close cooperation from the community, has from its inception in 1872 worked to see that Fayette schools rank in the top tier of the state's school systems, scoring high over the years in standardized testing and earning Schools of Excellence and National Blue Ribbon honors.

The stated mission of the school system is to deliver "effective instruction and set high expectations, resulting in continued improvement in student achievement."

Fayette's first school was established in 1824 with the opening of the Fayetteville Academy, which would later bring fame to the county in the 1930s.

In 1857 the co-ed Fayetteville Seminary was created with facilities for students to board in town at a cost of $9 a month. One momentous occasion recorded in the *Fayetteville News* was the destruction of the Academy building in 1892 by a strong wind, which the paper called a "cyclone." The building also gained fame in the opening pages of Margaret Mitchell's epic classic, "Gone with the Wind," where Scarlett attended the "Fayetteville Female Academy." In fact, Mitchell's grandmother and her grandmother's sisters boarded in Fayetteville and attended the school.

As the county's population grew over the years, so did its schools. Today, 30 schools make up the Fayette County School System, including

17 elementary; 6 middle; 5 high; 1 alternative high; and 1 evening high. Another new elementary school, Rivers, will be open fall 2009.

The stellar reputation of the school system helps it attract the best teachers to its classrooms. Talented teachers, coupled with parental and community involvement, enable the Fayette County School System to offer its students an excellent educational experience.

The school system's strong commitment to providing a well rounded education for all students correlates to its vision of producing students capable of living and working effectively, responsibly and productively in a global environment.

In 1997, Fayette Community Hospital opened as a 100-bed facility on the 22-acre campus between Fayetteville and Peachtree City after concentrated community efforts that began in the 1980s.

Many Fayette community and government leaders worked to bring to fruition the hospital, which in 2004 was renamed Piedmont Fayette Hospital (PFH), to more clearly align it with the parent company, Piedmont Healthcare.

Among local leaders spearheading the hospital effort in the early 1990s was Fayette Chamber President, Ron Duffey. In 1995, W. Darrell Cutts was named president and CEO after a twenty-year career at Piedmont Hospital in Atlanta. Geraldine Stinchcomb, Fayette County's first public health nurse and a graduate of the Piedmont Hospital School of Nursing, who has volunteered more than 1,500 hours, was there to greet guests the first day the hospital opened. The first board chairman was Dr. Mark Pentecost.

Since its inception the hospital hospital has grown to a 143-bed, acute care facility serving the heart of Fayette and the southern crescent. It incorporates the best ideas from architecture to technology, quality, and patient safety, emphasizing a balance between health and care. Piedmont Fayette Hospital's wide range of services includes:

• Medical and surgical services;
• 24-hour emergency services;
• Diagnostic and Imaging services;

• Rehabilitation and Fitness Services; and
• Internal medicine physician services.

Hospital, physicians and staff have earned many honors and awards. PFH proudly displays the Gold Seal of Approval™ awarded by the

Joint Commission to accredited organizations. In 2007, for the fourth consecutive year, PFH was named one of the nations' 100 *Top Hospitals*, which recognizes hospitals that are the highest performers in the nation based on objective statistical performance measurements across five critical areas: clinical outcomes, patient safety, operational efficiency, financial performance and growth in patient volume. In 2008, for the fourth year, PFH was named one of the nation's "Most Wired" hospitals, which focus on the use of information technologies for quality, customer service, public health and safety, business process and workforce issues.

PFH has also been awarded for quality and patient safety for its initiatives, one entitled "Reduction of Blood Culture Contamination Rates." By reducing the rate, it increases the accuracy of pathogen identification and reduces exposing patients to unnecessary antibiotics that can lead to the development of drug resistant organisms and increased length of stay costs.

DESIGN COMPONENTS, INC.

Clockwise from top, left: John Fox (left), president from 1978 to 1996; Jay Woods, vice president from 1978 to 1989; Mark Sparrow, vice president from 1996 to present; and James Fox, president from 1996 to present.

Design Components, Inc. (DCI), has been a leader in the design, engineering, and distribution of metal building accessories since 1978.

DCI can actually trace its beginnings to the early 1970s with Jay Woods, who had a knack for sales, and John Fox, whose background was engineering. The two became manufacturer's representatives, marketing gravity ventilators, gutters, down spouts, specialty flashings, and sealants to metal building manufacturers and contractors.

This original team went into business as Woods & Fox Associates and later adopted the name Design Components as the company's role developed beyond mere sales and into the actual design of products.

In the mid-1970s, there was a growing need for more sophisticated roof systems and DCI became an integral part of the design and marketing of one of the first Standing Seam Roof Systems utilizing an automatic seaming machine.

In the early 1980s, metal buildings became more specialized and less "pre-engineered." As building owners began to put mechanical equipment on the roofs, a need arose for roof penetration products. To fill this need, DCI marketed die-formed plastic roof jacks for pipe penetrations and die-formed plastic roof curbs with a galvanized steel sub-frame to support fans and vents.

In the mid-1980s, DCI became one of the first companies to market custom fabricated metal roof curbs, as well as flexible EPDM rubber pipe flashings. Later in the decade, DCI helped introduce a roof top walkway system to provide roof protection and personal safety while walking on roofs. Today, DCI sells its trademarked METALWALK system with an optional safety handrail.

Fox served as president of the company from 1978 to 1996, and was succeeded by his son, James Fox. Woods was vice president from 1978 until 1989 and that position is now filled by Mark Sparrow.

The company, located at 115 Walter Way, has been located in Fayetteville since 1996. Gross annual sales have grown from $160,000 in 1978 to more than $3 million in 2008 and the firm expects continued steady growth through more aggressive marketing to both domestic and foreign contractors and building owners.

Formally established in 1967, the Fayette County Chamber of Commerce has a long and proud record as the "Voice of Business" in the Fayette community.

The foundation was initiated by a core group of Fayette County Jaycees and businessmen including Jimmy Cooper, Toby Cooper, Sam Jones, Hewlette Harrell, Crawford Hewell and Don Scarbrough who met to discuss the concept at the American Legion in Fayetteville in 1965. Founding members also included Crawford Bailey, Huie Bray, David Carnes, James Conner, Edward Davis, Floy Farr, Claude Goza, Ray Hensley, Esric Lee, Derrel Martin, C.J. Mowell, Jr., Neal Nunnally, Clarence Stanley and J.M. Vickery.

In February 1967 the Chamber organization was established at a meeting in which Crawford Hewell was elected president. The charter and by-laws were written by J.M. Vickery. Soon after the Chamber's first logo was created by artist Bill Cawthorne. The board of directors held its first full meeting in March 1967 in the civic room of the Fayetteville Farmers and Merchants Bank.

Carolyn Cary volunteered as the executive secretary for many years, conducting Chamber business from her home in Fayetteville for the first four years. She has continued her extensive service serving as the historian and documenting and preserving much of its history.

In the 1960s, Cary published the first brochure for the chamber featuring twenty-five new industries, new houses and a shopping center "coming soon." After several years, progress was made and today the site is occupied by the stores located by Michael's in Fayetteville. The first groundbreaking ceremony was in 1968 when Tri-City Federal Savings and Loan, currently Region's Bank, was built next to the Holiday-Fife house on West Lanier.

To support the community the chamber entered a sophomore at Georgia College, Becky Smith (Hughes), in the "Stay and See Georgia" contest. It also encouraged various Homemaker Clubs to have anti-litter campaigns, plant flowers at the Courthouse and back former mayor, A. O. "Bo" Ingram in creating the Jack Day Park at the corner of Highway 54 East and Highway 85 South. Jack Day was a popular pharmacist in Fayetteville until his untimely death in the early 1970s. In 1996, Jack Day Park became known as Heritage Park.

In June 1968 the chamber published its first newsletter, *The Communicator*. Hewlette Harrell was then the second president and stressed in the president's column the importance of obtaining new industry in the community. A different business in the county was spotlighted in those first newsletters and the first one was "Hi Brand Foods" who had been in the county seven years at that time. The building was eventually demolished in 2002 and The Avenue shopping center is now located on that site.

A dozen determined people literally held the Chamber together for those first tenuous years—good ideas and good people evolved into the vibrant organization the chamber is today.

In the spring of 1996 the Fayette County Chamber of Commerce relocated into the Old Courthouse building at 200 Courthouse Square in Fayetteville, where it remains today. Available at www.FayetteChamber.org, you will find additional information on the chamber, member businesses, current events, job opportunities, newcomer's information and much more.

❖

COURTESY OF THE COLLECTION OF THE FAYETTE COUNTY HISTORICAL SOCIETY.

TRIDENT PET/CT OF FAYETTE

Above: The medical imaging team in front of their new Siemens PET/CT scanner.

Below: The liver images are CT Scan and PET/CT Scan of patient with liver cancer (bright orange dot in middle of liver).

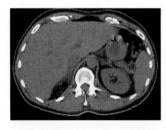

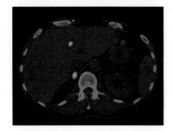

Since its founding in 2003 Fayette's Trident Medical Imaging Center has provided thousands of cancer patients the vital service of proper diagnosis leading to appropriate treatments, which provides a dramatically improved quality of life.

"The proper diagnosis and staging of a patient's cancer is critical in developing an appropriate treatment specific for each patient," explained Ken Manning, one of the founders and now Chief Operating Officer of TMI. Other owners and founders are CEO and President Fred Stuvek, Jr., and Chief Financial Officer Guy Messer. Each of the founders has a strong medical background in both clinical settings and the medical manufacturing area, thus providing a firm foundation for the company.

TMI now consists of six sites including its Savannah operation. Other locations are two in Lawrenceville, one in Alpharetta and Woodstock, and the corporate office and center in Fayetteville. "We offer convenient parking, same day scheduling, immediate registration and twenty-four-hour results," says Manning. "And we have the benefit of a network, with better access for more patients." Available at www.tridentmedicalimaging.com you will find an abundance of information including map with locations near you and even driving directions.

TMI has become a leader in outpatient diagnostic imaging in Georgia. "Our plans are to continue this focus and expand our operations throughout the Atlanta metropolitan area so that our patient base and our referring physicians can find one of our facilities near every major community throughout the area," Messer pointed out. "Our patients are used to the kind and compassionate service we provide and our referring physicians have become accustomed to the efficient and timely turnaround of our diagnostic reports. We want them to have access to this continued level of service throughout the Atlanta area."

TMI has approximately sixty employees across Georgia and has annual revenues of close to $15 million.

"We place high value on the accuracy and quality of our product, the integrity and compassion of our staff and strive for continuous improvement in ongoing physician education and patient empowerment," concluded Stuvek.

Trident has proven to be a high-quality alternative to hospitals for high-end imaging services. "It's like going to your doctor's office, only faster," Manning says. "We're a comfortable, convenient and cost-effective alternative to hospital-based healthcare."

Trident Medical Imaging, 1275 Highway 54 West, Suite 102, Fayetteville, Georgia, 30214. 770-719-3754.

State Bank of Georgia, which opened on the major east-west corridor between Fayetteville and Peachtree City in 2007, adds an international flavor to the history of banking in Fayette County and Atlanta.

Organized by a diverse group of twenty-one business professionals, the board includes several Indian-Americans, including bank chairman, Dr. Chandler Sharma.

The idea to open a multi-cultural bank was born out of a "kitchen table" discussion. Chief Financial Officer Kevin Sharpe, a former regulator in the Department of Banking and Finance and past CFO at the Capital City Bank, felt there was a need for a minority owned bank in the area. He got together a group of two to three people who brought in other people from different communities. Along the way it made sense to change the thinking to building a culturally diverse bank rather than a minority bank.

"While most banks start off with a marginal unit or store front, State Bank of Georgia was fortunate to find the perfect building to house the bank off Gingercake Road in Fayetteville. From the tastefully done interiors of the building an energetic group of professionals

promote 'relationship banking'" said CEO Jerry Stapleton. "Our people are trained to learn about you and your family and to analyze your needs."

Speaking of the Bank's customer philosophy he added, "We are not order takers. We actually do care and provide personal attention to each customer." As an example, SBG has a sunset rule where all phone calls and emails receive a response before the end of the day. "I am as accessible as anybody else at the bank," says Stapleton.

The top five bank officers have a total of 160 years of banking experience.

"We know what it takes to compete in an arena of mega-banks. We have recruited the finest talent in banking because we know that to be successful we have to have good people. We have seasoned commercial and consumer lenders as well as seasoned mortgage lenders," Stapleton adds.

"SBG's marketing strategy is to be a little bit better than other community banks," says Lydia Morris, senior retail and marketing manager. She prides herself in remembering every customer's name.

❖

Above: State Bank of Georgia's customer lobby, representing a traditional timeless look for a progressive community bank.

Below: (From left to right) Lydia Morris, senior vice president, retail and marketing; Eileen Kempf, senior vice president, operations; Jerry Stapleton, president and CEO; Mike Teal, chief lending officer; and Kevin Sharpe, senior vice president and CFO.

ACREAGE TO EDEN, INC.

❖

From top to bottom: Fayette Amphitheater, Town Square Jewelers, Old National Medical Building, and the Church Of Christ.

As indicated by the name of his firm, architect John Reeves, considers his business an extension of his commitment to follow God's will in his life. His mission statement is based on a verse in I Corinthians: "Whatever we do, we do it all for the glory of God." And his personal and professional goals are to "Serve the client first, providing innovative design solutions that meet environmental, safety, and cost considerations."

While paying for his education, Reeves had many different jobs—from selling linens to operating heavy equipment—and was working as the regional vice president of a Fortune 500 company before turning his full attention to architecture.

After passing the Architectural Exam on the first attempt, Reeves decided to concentrate on his own firm. Although he had little money and his wife was pregnant, "God blessed us and sent plenty of clients to our door," he explained.

Reeves first came to Fayetteville in 1988 performing ministry work through Lisbon Baptist Church, working in Atlanta firms and doing local residential and landscape design. Acreage To Eden was founded in 1997, and now offers full service architectural and construction services to both commercial and residential clients. Over the years, Reeves has completed over 500 projects throughout the nation, including a current project, Town Square Jewelers in Fayetteville for which he was also the contractor.

Other local projects include Wisdom Pointe Center, which received the Building of the Year Award from the Peachtree City Mayor, J&R Clothing, Inman Methodist, Timberlake, Tara Credit, and St. Mark Lutheran.

As an inventor he currently has his own beach access stair patent pending under Beachway, Inc., and has been trusted to be involved in invention designs and patent drawings, business development, and logo development for other clients.

As director of Leadership Fayette, Reeves spurred ministries like landmark restoration, and F. C. Jail Ministry Board, which provides inmates with their GED.

Looking to the future, Reeves says his business plan calls for him, "To be aware of the community's needs and to be in tune with God's plan."

Heritage of Peachtree is a calm oasis amidst the hustle and bustle of daily life. Soothing music plays in the comfortable living room, delicious meals are served restaurant-style in the lovely dining room and many interesting activities are offered throughout each day.

Originally named Peachtree Manor, the name was changed to Heritage of Peachtree in the late 1990s following the sale of the property. Over the years, Heritage of Peachtree has gained a reputation for exceptional customer service and a sincere love and concern shown to each resident.

This comfortable community was built in 1995 by Peachtree City residents Richard Krauth and son, Scott. Containing forty-eight one bedroom apartments, all on the ground floor, the Heritage property provides a home-like atmosphere that is soothing to both residents and visitors alike.

Consistently setting industry standards for resident care, activities, food service and overall satisfaction, Heritage now finds itself at the forefront of a new wave of smaller, more intimate retirement communities geared toward a more personal approach to senior living.

Seniors who no longer want to live on their own love the concept of having a twenty-four hour staff on call in case of emergencies. In addition, three home-style meals each day and transportation around town draw residents as do the numerous activities.

This well designed community has many innovative features suited to a senior resident. In the garden a wide diversity of trees and shrubs carefully chosen for their wildlife attraction provides nesting areas for dozens of bird species, while a wide walking path allows residents to spend time outdoors bird watching. A beautiful screened porch offers residents a comfortable place to rock away a summer afternoon while several covered verandas and decks afford alternative seating areas.

Heritage of Peachtree is presently owned by Royal Senior Care, a Miami based senior care provider. Located along Highway 54 West, Heritage is just at the edge of Peachtree City, convenient to both Fayetteville and Peachtree City.

THE OLIVET CHURCH

The history of Fayetteville's Olivet Baptist Church of Christ is inseparable from the Creecy family's one hundred year legacy of continuous leadership and commitment to the Christian ministry.

It was in 1979 when the Reverend Dr. Howard Creecy, Sr., and his son Howard, Jr., had a vision for a new church, which in 1991 opened its doors as The Olivet Baptist Church of Christ with Dr. Creecy, Sr., as founding pastor.

The son of a prominent New Orleans pastor, Dr. Creecy, Sr., who holds degrees from Alabama State University, Union Theological Seminary in New Orleans, Morehouse School of Religion and Atlanta's Interdenominational Theological Center, followed in his father's, Reverend W.W. Creecy, footsteps by serving in many religious and civic capacities nationally prior to founding The Olivet Church.

Dr. Creecy, Jr., the third generation pastor in the family, served for twenty-six years as senior pastor of Atlanta's Saint Peter Missionary Baptist Church before, in 2002, joining the leadership team with his father at Olivet.

Dr. Creecy, Jr., along with his wife and partner in ministry, Yolanda, assumed the full leadership mantle from Dr. Creecy as his health began to fail.

A graduate of Morehouse College and with a Doctor of Divinity from Abotra Bible Institute and Seminary, Dr. Creecy is involved in numerous civic, social and political activities.

"Our mission at Olivet is to provide a place where people will have a life-changing experience with God. Our vision is to provide a 'Church Home' where believers grow to become Disciples of Christ who are dedicated to Christian service," Dr. Creecy emphasized.

Olivet's inaugural service took place in September 1991 at Fayetteville's Kenwood Christian Church and in the following October, forty-seven charter members officially established the church. The present location was purchased a few months later and in February 1992 the first worship service was held there.

In 1998 the church's first building expansion began which provided much needed space for Administration Christian Education, ministry training and activities, plus additional sanctuary seating to accommodate the three Sunday morning worship services.

The Olivet Church is located at 877 Highway 314 North in Fayetteville and on the Internet at www.theolivetchurch.org.

The Fayette County Courthouse

The Fayette Fund, a local branch of The Community Foundation for Greater Atlanta, was established in 1994 to focus specifically on the needs and interests of Fayette County citizens. The Fayette Fund is one of four local funds located within The Community Foundation's twenty-three county service area and the local Advisory Board is comprised of knowledgeable leaders representing diverse segments of the Fayette community.

The Fayette Fund is committed to developing and promoting local philanthropy. The organization works closely with nonprofit organizations, professional advisors, and community leaders to develop the connections that make philanthropy happen in Fayette County. Through its work, the Foundation encourages local expertise and knowledge of the community to direct more funding and support toward the issues that affect Fayette County.

The Fayette Fund established an annual grant program in 2003 for Fayette nonprofit organizations. Grant funds awarded from this program totaled more than $125,000 from 2003 through 2008. However, the financial impact to the Fayette community from both unrestricted and restricted grants through The Community Foundation is much greater and has totaled more than $570,000 from 2005 through 2007.

In addition, The Fayette Fund helps donors and their families meet their charitable goals by educating them on critical issues and by matching them with organizations that serve their interests. The Fund helps donors leave a lasting legacy for the benefit of the Fayette community through a variety of funds and giving options. Individuals and families set up donor-advised funds through The Community

Foundation and, in turn, receive very personalized service as well as effective administration of those funds.

Founding Advisory Board Chair Joel Cowan, who served from 1994 to 2007, comments that, "Working with The Community Foundation allows me to combine my passion for giving back with the deep knowledge of the community to improve our region today and in the future."

❖

Joel Cowan, Founding Advisory Board Chair of the Fayette Fund, served from 1994 to 2007. Mr. Cowan is also a former board member of The Community Foundation for Greater Atlanta.

The Community Foundation for Greater Atlanta, founded in 1951, connects donors, nonprofits, and community leaders to strengthen the Atlanta region. As one of the largest and fastest growing community foundations in the nation, The Community Foundation has assets totaling more than $750 million and awarded more than $90 million in grants in 2008.

For more information, visit The Community Foundation for Greater Atlanta's website at www.cfgreateratlanta.org.

BULLDOG SUPPLY, INC.

E. J. Miller (1921-2005), founder of Bulldog Supply, Inc., spent many years honing his skills as a master soap and, later, snack salesman traveling the northeast in his younger days. It was not until he began to pursue a long time dream of owning a small business near his home that he began to realize true success. In his later years he confided to his grandson, J. H. Hooper, now president of Bulldog Supply, "All I really ever wanted was a small business that would allow me to stay close to home and make a living."

In 1978, taking advantage of Eddie's industrial knowledge and the unique characteristics of the Peachtree City golf car community, E. J. and his wife, Charlotte Miller (1928-2004), opened Bulldog Supply and began selling items to the local industry and Club Cars within the community. Operating with the slogan, "Service is our greatest asset,"

❖

Above: E. J. and Charlotte Miller, founders of Bulldog Supply.

Below: Jonathan and J. H. Hooper.

the couple built a loyal customer base over the years.

The company rapidly grew from a two person operation and today is one of Fayette County's most recognizable companies. A milestone of thirty years in operation was just celebrated. Since its inception Bulldog Supply has always been a family business and is now run by the Miller grandsons, the aforementioned J. H., who joined the company in 1992, and Jonathan Hooper, who has been with Bulldog since 1997.

Bulldog Supply has valued its association with Club Car over the years. They sell new, remanufactured and used golf cars for individual families and for local industry. Both golf cars and XRT all terrain vehicles are sold. A large rental fleet is maintained and is in use all over the Atlanta area. "We also have a great staff of professional mechanics, service providers and sales associates that see to it that our customer service is second to none," J. H. Hooper says.

"Our mission remains to create true value for our customers by offering quality products backed by superior service and competitive pricing," Hooper concluded.

Bulldog Supply, Inc., is located at 142 Huddleston Road in Peachtree City and at www.bulldogsupply.com.

AIS COMPUTERS

Alpha Information Systems, dba AIS Computers, was founded in 1982 by Tommy Turner, Jim Seigle, and Clark Schadle. They began the business by selling Franklin Computers, an Apple clone. After a few years the competitive edge of the Franklin started to decline with the introduction of the Apple IIE. The partners applied for and were awarded an Apple dealership in 1984.

AIS employees have been involved in a wide variety of community activities, including the Fayette County Chamber of Commerce, Fayette Senior Services, Fayette Community Foundation, Metro Fayette Kiwanis, Piedmont Fayette Hospital and many others. AIS Community Liaison, Vicki Turner, served as Board Chair of the Fayette County Chamber of Commerce in 2004 and received the organization's Business Person of the Year Award in 2006.

AIS Computers, an Apple Specialist, has been selling and servicing Apple Computers for over twenty years. As an Authorized Apple Reseller and Service Provider, AIS offers the full product line of Apple hardware and software. AIS accepts Mac trade-ins and provides reconditioned pre-owned sales thus offering clients valuable alternatives. AIS can repair Macs both in-warranty and out-of-warranty. Additional repair services are

provided for PCs out-of-warranty, and select iPods out-of-warranty.

In July 2008, AIS was purchased by Computer Advantage, Inc., out of Sarasota, Florida. The AIS Fayetteville and Savannah locations currently operate with the dba AIS Computers. Computer Advantage, like AIS Computers, is an Apple Specialist with over twenty years experience on the Apple platform. The merging of AIS and Computer Advantage has allowed both companies to utilize their strengths and combine resources to better serve clients.

For more information about AIS Computers, please visit www.aiscomputers.com.

❖

Vicki Turner.

CHRIST OUR SHEPHERD LUTHERAN CHURCH

Fayette County native Jimmy Booth, longtime journalist and public relations practitioner, initiated the move that led to the formation of the Christ Our Shepherd Lutheran Church when he ran an ad in 1974 in his local newspaper, "This Week in Peachtree City," inviting people who were interested in a local Lutheran church to please contact him. He then sent a request to the national organization, Lutheran Church in America, for assistance.

That is when the Reverend John Weber, mission developer, came to town to "Knock on doors to develop a Lutheran Church" for Peachtree City.

When Reverend Weber arrived on the scene there were ten families who had expressed interest in a Lutheran Church. "I knocked on doors in the city and surrounding area until June 1975," Reverend Weber recalls. "Ninety-five people signed a charter."

Reverend Weber remembers, "At the time there were only a few other churches in the planned city, including Baptist, Presbyterian and Methodist." He continued to knock on doors until the charter was signed, giving impetus to the new church.

Citing those who played important roles in the Church's founding, Reverend Weber said, "The key people included Howard and Geneva Bourdeau, who still live in Peachtree City. Howard was the congregation's first president. Other key leaders were Rod and Danee Burkow and Ted and Sandy Thomas and their young children."

Reverend Weber early on bonded with the community becoming involved with the Peachtree City volunteer fire department and training as an emergency medical technician. He was the first paramedic in Fayette County.

The Church completed its first building in July 1978. "It has always been a mission for the Church to be used for ministry to the community, opening its doors to AA, Alanon and many other support organizations," Reverend Weber points out.

Since its founding Christ Our Shepherd has gone through two more building programs and launched two other Lutheran congregations, one in Fayetteville and one in Newnan. At present it has a membership of 1,800 and five worship services on the weekend.

After operating his D. A. C. A. Roofing company for more than two decades in his native Europe, Luc Vandebuerie moved the company to the U.S. in 1998 after marrying "...a lovely Kansas woman" he met on a business trip to this country.

A native of Belgium, Luc honed his considerable skills working a variety of jobs all over the continent and for fifteen years specialized in the restoration of historical sites. He attended roofing college for eight years to become qualified to install the many different kinds of roofs prevalent in Europe. Speaking of his training he said, "We were required to know not only how to install a roof, but also about the material we work with, how it is manufactured, what it is made of and its characteristics so we can understand why certain roofs are installed the way they are."

Shawna Vandebuerie, that "lovely Kansas woman," is a champion of her husband's work. "Since he went to roofing and business school for eight years, one could say he has a PhD in roofing. Much of his work in Europe involved his special skills doing roof restoration of centuries-old churches, castles and forums. He is a true student of his craft who uses simple logic in solving complex roofing problems."

Roofing is a family affair with the Vandebueries. Two of his sons are roofers in Europe and one works with Luc in this country.

The Fayetteville company, located at 160-A Robinson Drive, combines established European roofing techniques and state-of-the-art roofing products and practices to provide superior roofing systems for both commercial and residential properties. Commenting on the skills he acquired in Europe, Luc said, "All good American roofers know how to install a roof according to its specifications, but not all know why those specifications are set. This additional knowledge helps D. A. C. A. find just the right type of roof to last through any weather conditions the customer's home or business might experience. This is how we give our customers better quality for the cost and stand behind the company's work one hundred percent."

D. A. C. A. serves both residential and commercial customers in Georgia, the Midwest, and the Southeast. Included in its work is everything from gutters to chimneys. The company's residential and commercial offerings include custom made copper and zinc roofs, siding and gutters, natural and synthetic slate, clay and concrete tile, roof ornaments and commercial PVC and TPO membrane.

For more information about D. A. C. A. Roofing, visit www.dacaroofing.com.

Above: A Spanish tile roof.

Below: Designs in slate.

ALLIED HEALTHCARE CLINICS

Above: Dr. Thomas, just before running the world's most difficult marathon at The Great Wall in China.

Below: Dr. John N. Thomas, D.C.

It's not just that he ran a marathon. There are many marathon runners in Fayette County. And it's not that he ran what's known as the most difficult marathon in the world, The Great Wall Marathon. It is that he did it five weeks after sustaining a bulging disc while training.

Dr. John N. Thomas, D.C., knew what to do when he hurt his back. He treated his back diligently, daily, with IDD Therapy®, something he specializes at his office, Allied Healthcare Clinics.

Known locally as The Running Doctor, Dr. Thomas opened Allied Healthcare Clinics more than a decade ago. He relocated his office to Fayetteville four years ago. He and his staff of professionals treat all of Fayette County for sports injuries and athletic performance optimization, as well as chiropractic care and physical and massage therapy. Recently, Dr. Thomas acquired the latest in spinal decompression technology, IDD Therapy®.

IDD Therapy® is a non-invasive procedure that has an eighty-six percent success rate in treating herniated, bulging, degenerated discs, sciatica, low back and neck pain and other similar conditions. Allied Healthcare Clinics are the only local certified and licensed facility for this treatment.

Because Dr. Thomas knew how to treat the kind of injury he suffered, he was able to utilize IDD Therapy® with astounding results. Finishing The Great Wall marathon was a huge victory for him. Back home, Dr. Thomas has seen impressive results from nearly every person he's treated with IDD Therapy®, from both athletes and less active patients.

Back pain is not the only reason why so many professional and amateur athletes see The Running Doctor. Dr. Thomas said, "Runners and athletes, in general, experience many different types of injuries ranging from illio-tibial band syndrome, plantar fasciitis and Achilles tendonitis to shoulder problems, back pain and headaches. We see hundreds of runners and triathletes that come in with all kinds of stuff from working their legs during marathons or riding 100 miles at a time on their fancy $5,000, 13-pound carbon fiber road bikes. And the crash victims … they are just lucky to be alive!"

Allied Healthcare Clinics sees more patients due to running injuries than from heavy lifting. When asked why, Dr. Thomas explained, "My practice is located in the heart of one of the nation's most active running and triathlon communities. We appeal to the runner and triathlete because of the services we offer and our understanding of the sport specific injuries that we see."

Dr. Thomas is a Board Certified Sports Chiropractor and is a professional member of the Georgia Chiropractic Association. He is an expert in his field in the area of conservative but comprehensive non-surgical care of spinal and disc injuries with spinal decompression.

For more information on Allied Healthcare Clinics and IDD Therapy® visit proven-back-pain-relief.com, or for sports related treatment by The Running Doctor see runningpainfree.com. Dr. Thomas offers free consultations by appointment. Call 770-460-1911 for details.

SPONSORS

ABOUT THE AUTHOR

CAROLYN CARY

A native of Ohio, Carolyn Cary has called Fayette County, "home" for over forty years. Ms. Cary has served as the official Fayette County historian since 1981. She was a founding member of the Fayette County Historical Society and Fayette County Chamber of Commerce, and served as the Chamber's first executive secretary. She is a past president of the Georgia Writer's Association. She wrote *William Thomas Overby: Proud Partisan Ranger* (2004) and edited *The History of Fayette County, 1821-1971* (1977). She is also a contributor to *The Citizen News*.

The recipient of numerous awards, Ms. Cary is extremely proud of having been chosen to be an Olympic torchbearer for the 1996 Olympics. She carried the torch into Heritage Park in Fayetteville, a park she had helped create.

ABOUT THE COVER

VICKI TURNER

Vicki Turner, established artist, has thirty-six years of experience in art and design. For the past twenty-five years she has been the creative side of AIS Computers. She has painted in oils, acrylics and watercolor for almost forty years and has displayed her art in local banks, bookstores and galleries in Georgia and Tennessee; she is best known for her attention to detail.

Turner was chosen by Congressman Lynn Westmoreland to paint a special ornament for the White House's "State" Christmas tree for 2008. She traveled to Washington, D.C., to represent Georgia and attended the artist reception hosted by First Lady Laura Bush.

Turner has a love for her community and has been volunteering for over twenty-five years in Fayette County. She and her husband Tommy have lived in Fayette County for thirty-five years and have two grown daughters.

She is honored to have her artwork on the cover.

For more information about the following publications or about publishing your own book, please call
Historical Publishing Network at 800-749-9790 or visit www.lammertinc.com.

Black Gold: The Story of Texas Oil & Gas

Garland: A Contemporary History

Historic Abilene: An Illustrated History

Historic Alamance County: An Illustrated History

Historic Albuquerque: An Illustrated History

Historic Amarillo: An Illustrated History

Historic Anchorage: An Illustrated History

Historic Austin: An Illustrated History

Historic Baldwin County: A Bicentennial History

Historic Baton Rouge: An Illustrated History

Historic Beaufort County: An Illustrated History

Historic Beaumont: An Illustrated History

Historic Bexar County: An Illustrated History

Historic Birmingham: An Illustrated History

Historic Brazoria County: An Illustrated History

Historic Charlotte:
An Illustrated History of Charlotte and Mecklenburg County

Historic Cheyenne: A History of the Magic City

Historic Comal County: An Illustrated History

Historic Corpus Christi: An Illustrated History

Historic DeKalb County: An Illustrated History

Historic Denton County: An Illustrated History

Historic Edmond: An Illustrated History

Historic El Paso: An Illustrated History

Historic Erie County: An Illustrated History

Historic Fairbanks: An Illustrated History

Historic Gainesville & Hall County: An Illustrated History

Historic Gregg County: An Illustrated History

Historic Hampton Roads: Where America Began

Historic Hancock County: An Illustrated History

Historic Henry County: An Illustrated History

Historic Houston: An Illustrated History

Historic Illinois: An Illustrated History

Historic Kern County:
An Illustrated History of Bakersfield and Kern County

Historic Lafayette:
An Illustrated History of Lafayette & Lafayette Parish

Historic Laredo:
An Illustrated History of Laredo & Webb County

Historic Lee County: The Story of Fort Myers & Lee County

Historic Louisiana: An Illustrated History

Historic Midland: An Illustrated History

Historic Montgomery County:
An Illustrated History of Montgomery County, Texas

Historic Ocala: The Story of Ocala & Marion County

Historic Oklahoma: An Illustrated History

Historic Oklahoma County: An Illustrated History

Historic Omaha:
An Illustrated History of Omaha and Douglas County

Historic Orange County:
The Story of Orlando & Orange County

Historic Ouachita Parish: An Illustrated History

Historic Paris and Lamar County: An Illustrated History

Historic Pasadena: An Illustrated History

Historic Passaic County: An Illustrated History

Historic Pennsylvania An Illustrated History

Historic Philadelphia: An Illustrated History

Historic Prescott:
An Illustrated History of Prescott & Yavapai County

Historic Richardson: An Illustrated History

Historic Rio Grande Valley: An Illustrated History

Historic Scottsdale: A Life from the Land

Historic Shelby County: An Illustrated History

Historic Shreveport-Bossier:
An Illustrated History of Shreveport & Bossier City

Historic South Carolina: An Illustrated History

Historic Smith County: An Illustrated History

Historic Temple: An Illustrated History

Historic Texarkana: An Illustrated History

Historic Texas: An Illustrated History

Historic Victoria: An Illustrated History

Historic Tulsa: An Illustrated History

Historic Williamson County: An Illustrated History

Historic Wilmington & The Lower Cape Fear:
An Illustrated History

Historic York County: An Illustrated History

Iron, Wood & Water: An Illustrated History of Lake Oswego

Miami's Historic Neighborhoods: A History of Community

Old Orange County Courthouse: A Centennial History

Plano: An Illustrated Chronicle

The New Frontier:
A Contemporary History of Fort Worth & Tarrant County

The San Gabriel Valley: A 21st Century Portrait

The Spirit of Collin County

Water, Rails & Oil: Historic Mid & South Jefferson County